Grief in Our Seasons

A MOURNER'S KADDISH COMPANION

Rabbi Kerry M. Olitzky

JEWISH LIGHTS PUBLISHING
Woodstock, Vermont

Grief in Our Seasons: A Mourner's Kaddish Companion

Library of Congress Cataloging-in-Publication Data

Olitzky, Kerry M.
    Grief in our seasons : a mourner's kaddish companion / by Kerry M. Olitzky.
        p.   cm.
    ISBN 1-879045-55-9 (pbk.)
    1. Consolation (Judaism)—Meditations. 2. Bereavement—Religious aspects—Judaism—Meditations. 3. Bible. O.T.—Meditations. 4. Jewish meditations. I. Title.
BM729.C6043   1997
296.4'45—dc21   97–35986
                                                          CIP

First edition

ISBN 1-879045-55-9 (Paperback)

10 9 8 7 6 5 4 3 2 1

Manufactured in the United States of America

Text design: Sans Serif, Inc.
Jacket design: Karen Savary
Jacket art: Eternal Light D.695, © 1988 by Kurt J. Matzdorf, Silversmith, Inc.

Published by Jewish Lights Publishing
A Division of LongHill Partners, Inc.
Sunset Farm Offices, Route 4
P.O. Box 237
Woodstock, Vermont 05091
Tel: (802) 457-4000 Fax: (802) 457-4004
www.jewishlights.com

For Debbie Friedman,
who has the heart of a poet
and the soul of a sage,
whose words and music
have formed a foundation for our journey home.

In memory of
Lillian Matlins and Antonio Bonanno,
whose deaths, and lives,
caused us to understand the need
for this companion to the mourning process.

Grateful acknowledgment is made for permission to reprint from the following works:

Felix Adler, *Creed and Deed*, New York: G. P. Putnam's Sons, 1850; Morris Adler, *May I Have a Word with You?* New York: Crown, 1967; Dr. Eugene Borowitz, *The Centenary Perspective*, New York: Central Conference of American Rabbis, 1976; "The death of those close to our hearts . . ." © by Nancy Gossels and Peter Gossels from *Vetaher Libenu* as published by Congregation Beth El of the Sudbury River Valley, 1980; Rabbi Alvin I. Fine, *Gates of Prayer*, New York: Central Conference of American Rabbis, 1975; and his "To the Living—" © Cong. Emanu-El of San Francisco; Freema Gottlieb, *The Lamp of God: A Jewish Book of Light*, Northvale, NJ: Jason Aronson, 1989. Reprinted by permission of the publisher, Jason Aronson Inc., Northvale, NJ © 1989; Arthur Green and Rabbi Marcia Praeger, *Kol Haneshamah*, PA: Reconstructionist Press, 1989; Rabbi Sidney Greenberg, *Words to Live By: Selected Writings,* Northvale, NJ: Jason Aronson, Inc., 1990. Reprinted by permission of the publisher, Jason Aronson Inc., Northvale, NJ © 1990; *Mahzor for Rosh Hashanah and Yom Kippur*, edited by Rabbi Jules Harlow. Copyright by the Rabbinical Assembly, 1972; Rabbi Abraham Joshua Heschel, *Moral Grandeur and Spiritual Audacity*, ed. Susannah Heschel, New York: Farrar, Straus and Giroux, 1996 © Estate of Abraham Joshua Heschel, Sylvia Heschel, Executrix; Harold Kushner, *When Bad Things Happen to Good People*, New York: Schocken Books, 1989 © 1981, 1989 by Harold S. Kushner; Rabbi Jakob Petuchowski, *Understanding Jewish Prayer*, Hoboken, NJ: KTAV Publishing Co., 1972; Rabbi Tzvi Rabinowicz, *A Guide to Life: Jewish Laws and Customs of Mourning*, Northvale, NJ: Jason Aronson, Inc., 1989. Reprinted by permission of the publisher, Jason Aronson Inc., Northvale, NJ © 1989; Rabbi Jack Riemer, *Jewish Reflections on Death*, New York: Schocken Books, 1976; (adaptation from) Rabbi Alexander M. Schindler, adapted from Editorial written by Rabbi Alexander M. Schindler, *Reform Judaism* 23, no. 2 (1994); Phyllis Toback, *The Invisible Thread: A Portrait of Jewish American Women* (Diana Bletter, Lori Grinker, eds.), Philadelphia: The Jewish Publication Society of America, 1989. Used by permission of the Jewish Publication Society.

Grateful acknowledgment is made in quoting from the following:

Rabbi Nina Cardin, Andrew Davids, Rabbi Harvey Fields, Rabbi Nancy Flam, Jeff Goldwasser, Rabbi Sam Gordon, Rabbi Tom Louchheim, Rabbi Bennett Miller, Dr. Carol Ochs, Rabbi Harold M. Schulweis, Rabbi Rami Shapiro, the estate of Mrs. A. Alan Steinbach, Rabbi Joseph Weiss.

Contents

How to Use This Book

Grief in Our Seasons is intended as a companion of comfort to saying Kaddish. It reflects the Jewish tradition of studying sacred texts while mourning and uniquely brings the elements of study and mourning together.

- Each section of the eleven major sections is devoted to a stage of mourning. You may want to follow the readings one section at a time or you may want to move from section to section depending on how you feel.

- Each section is divided into weekly chapters for your study and reflection.

- Since the Torah is the touchstone for Jewish study and spirituality, I have selected material from the Torah at the beginning of each week (on Sunday) and toward the end (on Friday). Likewise, on Shabbat, I have selected material from the prophetic literature (generally taken from various haftarah portions). Selections during intervening days (and holidays) are taken from the wide spectrum of Jewish literature. The process of selection had one guiding principle: Texts were selected to reflect a stage of mourning while offering you comfort, consolation, and understanding during your own journey. I have taken the liberty of translating the Hebrew in such a way as to make it as inclusive as possible. In this way, I hope that the sacred text might sing in the soul of all who read it.

- Space is provided each day for you to write your own reflections about your mourning and about the texts you study.

- At the end of each weekly section, I have also included a meditation to use daily.

However you use this book, keep in mind the memory of the one you have lost. On the inside of the back cover is guidance to take you through a ritual of reflection intended to enhance your study and affirm the memory of your deceased. Use the material in this book before or after you say Kaddish.

Personal Reflections— Creating a Book of Memory

After you read each day's entry, you may want to reflect on these words, and on your mourning, in writing. This then becomes a book of memory, similar to the memory books that evolved among our European brothers and sisters in the Middle Ages. It will provide you with the opportunity to review your thoughts throughout the year. In many cases, that's how rabbinic commentaries on these texts developed. But in this case, it will not take the schooling or training of a rabbi to do so—only your feeling heart.

A Meditation Before Saying Kaddish

Following every seven pages is a meditation—words that have been penned by someone else to help you reflect on the saying of Kaddish. I included it after Shabbat because most people go to the synagogue on Shabbat more regularly than during other times of the week. Because these selections are culled from the experiences of others who have faced the challenges of mourning, I believe that they will provide you with an extra measure of comfort.

Rabbi Kerry M. Olitzky

Preface

Saying Kaddish is part of the long and difficult process of mourning. It's something that Jewish tradition asks us to do and something we want to do. We do it for the one we loved who is now gone, and we do it to ease the pain of our loss. Mourning (*avelut*) helps move us from the immediate experience of raw grief (*aninut*) to slowly reentering the routine of daily living and ultimately accepting our loss. Since we cannot do this alone, Judaism buoys us throughout the period of mourning by insisting that we seek out community. While mourning is a personal experience, we usually give voice to our grief in the midst of a community through sitting shiva and by saying Kaddish each day in a minyan. These allow friends to reach out and comfort us by preparing our meals and helping us with daily chores until we are able to resume these tasks for ourselves.

Because daily life often loses its meaning in the face of death, in order to give us structure for our mourning, Jewish tradition has established a particular routine for saying Kaddish during the days, weeks, and months of mourning that follow the loss of someone we love. But saying Kaddish in a congregation or even in a minyan of ten people is not always possible. And even when there is a community in which to say Kaddish, some find it insufficiently supportive and comforting. So, in this companion to mourning, we offer something additional for you to do that—like Kaddish—may help ease the pain of mourning while constantly calling to mind the memory of the one who is gone.

Even in the face of death, Jewish tradition reminds us of our obligation to understand and affirm life. Such understandings and affirmations of life in the face of death never come quickly or easily. They do not come in predictable or orderly stages. While we may understand the phases of mourning, there are no well-tested formulas for solace that bring comfort the same way for each person. But Jewish ritual does anchor us through this process. Saying Kaddish is part of it. So are study, prayer, ritual, and memory.

If you can regularly say Kaddish as part of a minyan, then we encourage you to do so. The personal benefits you will receive are difficult to anticipate, but you will be rewarded by the experience. In addition to the words of Kaddish, consider the words in this volume; they will help moor you in Jewish tradition and life.

If you cannot regularly say Kaddish as part of a minyan, you can still do something each day to honor the memory of your loved one and to help yourself. Follow the pages of this companion. We will help you mourn, heal, remember, and accept your loss.

Move through this companion at your own pace. We have arranged its sections according to the stages of mourning as experienced by many people. But there is no correct pattern of mourning to follow. Therefore, we have left blank the actual dates for each day. Fill them in as you see fit. If you'd like, skip around according to the way you feel. Create your own sequence of reading as the emotions you experience take you into the various dimensions of your mourning.

Through specifically defined stages of mourning, Jewish ritual mirrors our movement through grieving as the sages understood it and gently moves the bereaved through a full range of emotions. While mourning, many of us experience a wide spectrum of emotions without warning. Although there is no pattern for individual mourning, the experience of others suggests that there are distinct stages of mourning. These frame the eleven sections of this book (which parallel the first eleven months of mourning, as prescribed by Jewish tradition): Denial, Disorganization, Anger, Guilt and Bargaining, Physical and Emotional Distress, Depression, Loss and Loneliness, Withdrawal, Acceptance, Healing, and Reaching Out. We also recognize that we often feel our loss more deeply during Jewish holidays when families often get together. Thus, we have an additional section for the major family-centered holidays in the Jewish calendar.

For a time, death removes the rational from us. Everything else in this world—*everything*—pales in the shadow of death. Our lives are radically changed as a result. No measure of sympathy can change that stark reality. From the moment we learn of the death of someone we love until we mark the *yahrzeit* anniversary of that death one year later, we are forced to reconstruct our lives. Time alone does not heal, and our pain will never fully subside. During the first year of mourning, we have to find a way to accept the changes that death has caused, so that we can come to terms with them and begin to develop a new routine for our lives. We have no alternative. We must do it. We owe it to ourselves—and to the memory of the one who died.

Rabbi Moses Leib of Sassov tells of a conversation heard between two local citizens in the community in which he lived. The first said, "Ivan, do you love me?" Came the response, "Of course, I love you." The friend pressed onward, "Ivan, do you know what gives me pain?" This time, Ivan said, "How can *I* know what gives *you* pain?" Distressed, the friend responded, "If you do not know what hurts me, then how can you say you love me?" Loving someone requires us to attempt to understand their pain; loving ourselves requires that we attempt to understand our own pain—and that we come to terms with it.

This book is a companion of comfort based on the insights of Jewish tradition. It has one goal in mind: to help you mourn by engaging in one of Judaism's most important activities—studying and thinking about sacred texts. When we immerse ourselves in the sacred texts of our people, we bring honor to the memory of the deceased and we drink from its healing waters.

With this companion, you will not only heal but learn about what Judaism teaches and about what it means to be a Jew. You will benefit from this for the rest of your life. This book is not intended to replace traditional Jewish mourning customs. The comfort of the minyan cannot be replaced by a solitary experience. But we hope to offer you levels of insight and healing that enhance the experience of saying Kaddish with or without a minyan. Simply put, it is here to help.

Acknowledgments

This book evolved over the course of a number of years. It is a prime example of partnership between publisher and author, both immersed in Jewish context and desirous of bringing Jewish content to the lives of people in mourning. So I thank Stuart and Antoinette Matlins, publishers of Jewish Lights Publishing, for joining me on the journey and remaining faithful to my work. These are two unique individuals whose dream has become a blessing for us all. I also want to thank my editor, Arthur Magida, who with an insightful pen carefully helped shape each thought into comforting words. I want to recognize the contributions of rabbinic students Andrew Davids and Jeff Goldwasser, who permitted me to add some of their thoughts along with my own and recommended the inclusion of other meditations as well. To all those whose words are included in these pages, I offer my humble thanks.

I specifically acknowledge the following individuals and publishers who have graciously given us permission to reprint their work among these pages: Rabbi Eugene B. Borowitz; Anne Brener; Rabbi Nina Beth Cardin; Rabbi Harvey Fields; Rabbi Alvin Fine; Rabbi Nancy Flam; Rabbi Neil Gillman; Rabbi Samuel N. Gordon; Nancy Gossels; Peter Gossels; Freema Gottlieb; Arthur Green; Rabbi Sidney Greenberg; Rabbi Harold Kushner; Rabbi Lawrence S. Kushner; Rabbi Richard Levy; Rabbi Thomas Louchheim; Carol Ochs; Rabbi Jonathan Omer-Man; Rabbi Marcia Praeger; Rabbi Jack Riemer; Rabbi

Rami Shapiro; Rabbi Alexander M. Schindler; Rabbi Harold Schulweis; and Rabbi Joseph I. Weiss.

Along the way, many people offered us guidance and insight from their own work in the Jewish community. While I am mindful that I risk forgetting to include some individuals, I am conscious of the need to acknowledge all of those who have helped bring this book to fruition. Individually, I thank Rabbis Jeffrey Ableser, Joe Black, Barnett Brickner, Nina Beth Cardin, Harry Danziger, Wayne Dosick, Michael L. Feshbach, Arnold G. Fink, Joseph M. Forman, Laura Geller, Samuel N. Gordon, Ronald Isaacs, Elliott Kleinman, Steven Kushner, Thomas Louchheim, Jeffrey Marx, Bennett F. Miller, Harry Rosenfeld, John Sherwood, Myra Soifer, Jonathan Stein, Cary D. Yales, Daniel G. Zemel; Cantor Jennifer Werby Levy; and Robert Nosanchuk.

On Saying Kaddish

Rabbi Akiva, who lived in the second century C.E., once saw a man struggling under a heavy load of wood. Rabbi Akiva stopped the man and said, "Why must you do this difficult work? If you are a slave and this labor is forced upon you, I will redeem you from your master and set you free. And if it is because you are poor and you must earn a living this way, I will make you rich." Frightened, the man responded, "Please let me go and do not detain me, so as not to anger those who are in charge of me."

The man's reply puzzled Rabbi Akiva, who asked, "Who are you and what is this all about?" To this, the man replied, "I am one of those unfortunate souls condemned to the agonies of hell-fire, and every day I am sent to bring my own wood for my own torment." "Is there then no way for you to be relieved of this suffering?" asked Akiva. "Yes," the man answered. "I heard that if my little son, whom I left behind, were to say in public, '*Yitgadal veyitkadash*' and the others would answer, '*Yehei Shemei rabba mevorakh*,' or if he were to say, '*Barekhu et Adonai hamevorakh*,' and the congregation would answer,'*Barukh Adonai hamevorakh l'olam va-ed*,' I would be set free from this judgment."

Akiva then asked the man for all the relevant details and promised to locate his child and teach him Torah so that he could stand in front of the congregation and say *Yitgadal* in praise of God. Akiva found the child and taught him Torah, the *Sh'ma*, the *Amidah*, and Grace After Meals and prepared him to stand before the congregation to recite *Yitgadal*. As soon as the boy did this, the father's soul was delivered from its judgment and permitted its eternal rest. The man then appeared to Akiva in a dream and thanked him: "May it be God's will that you rest in peace, for you made it possible for me to be at peace."

—Adapted from *Netiv Binah* I, pp. 367–68

To Say, or Not to Say, Kaddish

Rabbi Harvey Fields

There are times when I read the Kaddish list and wonder, "Where are the absent loved ones of these names? Are they so busy that they can't make the time to thank God for their mother or father, their sister or brother, their lost spouse or child?"

The wisdom of Jewish tradition prescribes the observance of *Yizkor* on Yom Kippur, Shemini Atzeret, Pesach, and Shavuot and the recitation of Kaddish at the *yahrzeit*, or yearly anniversary, of a loved one. Why?

Encountering death, says the Psalmist, helps us understand our fleeting place in existence. We are like a dream at daybreak. In the morning we are like grass growing green and fresh. In the evening we are cut down and decay: Our days are speedily gone, and we fly away. Confronting that truth about us charges us with the urgency of using the gift of our lives with wisdom.

Yet, in a way, that message seems obvious. After all, most of us know that we are fragile compounds of flesh and blood and that the clock of our life is running down from the time we are born.

So why say Kaddish if all we get out of it is a grim warning about wasting our precious years?

Because our loved ones want to be remembered by us just as we want others, when our times comes, to remember us. Moments of Kaddish uplift memories. They open up the albums of our relationships. They allow us to sift through the pictures, to recall the moments of laughter and triumph, pain and joy we shared. They plunge us into the successes and failures of those who meant the most to us and into measuring the signature of their lives left as an indelible imprint upon our souls.

We ought to be saying Kaddish and observing *Yizkor* because without our albums and memories we are incomplete. The portrait of our being is broken, fragmentary, deficient. We require our Kaddish memories to make us whole—but "whole" not just in tender recollections of our past but in the confrontation of how we are painting the portrait of what others will recall of us!

Saying Kaddish is also about dealing with how we will be remembered—or whether anyone will want to say Kaddish for us.

Will they recall our anger, arrogance, abuse, neglect, sarcasm, stinginess, or stubbornness? Or will they miss our love, long for our support, yearn for our kindness, wisdom, generosity, honesty—our warm arms of affection?

When they rise to say to say Kaddish for us, will they find us inside themselves, our gifts coiled into the particles and structures of their spirits?

Will our voices whisper to them, "When I am gone, look for me in the people I have known. When you miss me, let me look through your eyes, your mind, and your acts of kindness. When you want to honor me, use your powers to mend the broken hearts around you. When you wonder where I am, want to feel my presence, then give my love away"?

Saying Kaddish is for such a confrontation. Without it, we miss the right questions. With it, we never lose those we love, nor ourselves.

Mourner's Kaddish

יִתְגַּדַּל וְיִתְקַדַּשׁ שְׁמֵהּ רַבָּא בְּעָלְמָא דִּי בְרָא כִרְעוּתֵהּ, וְיַמְ־
לִיךְ מַלְכוּתֵהּ בְּחַיֵּיכוֹן וּבְיוֹמֵיכוֹן וּבְחַיֵּי דְכָל בֵּית יִשְׂרָאֵל, בַּעֲגָלָא
וּבִזְמַן קָרִיב, וְאִמְרוּ: אָמֵן.
יְהֵא שְׁמֵהּ רַבָּא מְבָרַךְ לְעָלַם וּלְעָלְמֵי עָלְמַיָּא!
יִתְבָּרַךְ וְיִשְׁתַּבַּח, וְיִתְפָּאַר וְיִתְרוֹמַם וְיִתְנַשֵּׂא, וְיִתְהַדָּר
וְיִתְעַלֶּה וְיִתְהַלָּל שְׁמֵהּ דְּקֻדְשָׁא, בְּרִיךְ הוּא, לְעֵלָּא מִן כָּל־
בִּרְכָתָא וְשִׁירָתָא, תֻּשְׁבְּחָתָא וְנֶחֱמָתָא דַּאֲמִירָן בְּעָלְמָא, וְאִמְרוּ:
אָמֵן.
יְהֵא שְׁלָמָא רַבָּא מִן שְׁמַיָּא וְחַיִּים עָלֵינוּ וְעַל כָּל יִשְׂרָאֵל
וְאִמְרוּ: אָמֵן.
עֹשֶׂה שָׁלוֹם בִּמְרוֹמָיו, הוּא יַעֲשֶׂה שָׁלוֹם עָלֵינוּ וְעַל כָּל
יִשְׂרָאֵל, וְאִמְרוּ: אָמֵן.

Yit-ga-dal ve-yit-ka-dash she-mei ra-ba be-al-ma di-ve-ra
khi-re-u-tei, ve-yam-likh mal-khu-tei be-cha-yei-khon u-ve-yo-mei-khon u-ve-cha-yei de-khol beit Yis-ra-eil, ba-a-ga-la u-vi-ze-man ka-riv, ve-i-me-ru: a-mein.

Ye-hei she-mei ra-ba me-va-rakh le-a-lam u-le-al-mei al-ma-ya.

Yit-ba-rakh ve-yish-ta-bach, ve-yit-pa-ar ve-yit-ro-mam
ve-yit-na-sei, ve-yit-ha-dar ve-yit-a-leh ve-yit-ha-lal she-mei de-ku-de-sha, be-rikh hu, le-ei-la min kol bi-re-kha-ta
ve-shi-ra-ta, tush-becha-ta ve-ne-che-ma-ta, da-a-mi-ran
be-al-ma, ve-i-me-ru: a-mein.

Ye-hei she-la-ma ra-ba min she-ma-ya ve-cha-yim a-lei-nu
ve-al kol Yis-ra-eil, ve-i-me-ru: a-mein.

O-seh sha-lom bim-ro-mav, hu ya-a-seh sha-lom a-lei-nu ve-al kol Yis-ra-eil, ve-I-me-ru: a-mein.

Let the glory of God be extolled. Let Your great name be hallowed, in the world whose creation You willed. May Your sovereign rule soon prevail, in our own day, our own lives, and the life of all Israel, and let us say: Amen.

Let Your great name be blessed forever and ever.

Let the name of the Holy Blessed One be glorified, exalted, and honored, although You are beyond all the praises, songs, and adorations that we can utter, and let us say: Amen.

For us and for all Israel, may the blessing of peace and the promise of life come true, and let us say: Amen.

May the One who makes peace in the high places, let peace descend on us, on all Israel, and let us say: Amen.

Psalm 23[*]

The Lord is my Shepherd; I shall not want
He maketh me to lie down in green pastures;
 He leadeth me beside still waters;
 He restoreth my soul;
 He guideth me in straight paths for His name's sake.
Yea, though I walk through the valley of the shadow of
 death,
 I will fear no evil,
 For Thou art with me
 Thy rod and Thy staff, they comfort me.
Thou preparest a table before me in the presence of mine
 enemies;
 Thou hast anointed my head with oil; my cup run-
 neth over.
Surely goodness and mercy shall follow me all the days of
 my life,
 And I shall dwell in the house of the Lord forever.

Psalm 23: An Alternative Translation

Adonai is my Shepherd; I lack nothing
You give me my ease in fertile pastures
 You lead me to drink in tranquil waters
 You renew my soul
 You guide me on straight paths for as befits Your
 reputation.

---

[*]This psalm is traditionally said by mourners, particularly during a
funeral service.

Even though I walk through the valley of the deepest
   darkness,
I will fear no evil
      For You are [always] with me.
Your comforting rod provides me solace.
You prepare a table for me [to eat at ease] in front of my
   enemies;
      My head oozes with oil; my cup is overflowing.
Surely merciful goodness will be mine throughout my life,
      And I will always remain in Adonai's precinct.

ONE

Denying Death

Barukh Dayan ha-emet.
Praised be the Righteous Judge.
—Words spoken by any Jewish person
hearing about the death of a person.

It's seldom an intentional act, but we deceive ourselves at many times in our lives. Somehow, we erroneously think that if we deny a certain aspect of reality, usually an unpleasant one, then we can will it out of existence. At the very least, we can make it go away for a time. Like Adam and Cain and other ancestors of ours, we play this spiritual survival game. Adam pretended that God could not find him in the Garden, and Cain feigned ignorance about the location of his brother. But eventually, when we least expect it, something forces us to confront the very thing that we are trying to disavow. In the meantime, we go to great lengths to accomplish this feat of self-deception, possibly even persuading others to participate with us in the myth we are weaving.

Our sages understood this predictable pattern of behavior, and the traditions they passed on to us resonate in the deepest reaches of the human soul. It's one of the reasons

1

why Jewish mourning rituals are so carefully constructed and provide us with such effective mooring. They are designed to help us directly confront things. Moreover, Jewish ceremonies help us gain a closer affinity to the Divine. This helps us when we are finally ready to confront a reality that is sometimes very painful; then we come to realize that we are never alone. Although we may have gained some comfort from our community, it is God Who is always at our side and provides us with the ultimate solace.

According to Halakhah (literally "the way to go"; the system of laws that provides structural guidance for Jews), a new mourner is initially freed from doing certain mitzvot. The rabbis who developed these guidelines understood the process of denial that we go through during the initial mourning period. Even when the death of a loved one is anticipated, the role of mourner comes unexpectedly upon us. As a result, the regular routine of life is turned upside down. This month's selections in *Grief in Our Seasons* will guide you through this period of mourning and offer you grounding and affirm you, just as it affirms the Foundation of all Life.

Isolation

Sunday/Yom Rishon _____ (today's date)

> *It is not good for a human to be alone.*
> —Genesis 2:18

*T*his is what the Torah text teaches us from nearly the first moment of Creation and certainly from the instant of our birth. We respond to this sacred mandate in a variety of ways. We establish loving relationships and build families and communities out of and around these relationships. Each supports the other. However, there are times—particularly when we mourn—that we want to be alone, when we want to separate ourselves from the community. And when a relationship has been abruptly severed through death, we feel as if we have been returned to the state of the primordial human: alone and isolated—even if we know that we, like our ancestors, are surrounded by the Garden and that God is tending to the flowers in it.

PERSONAL REFLECTIONS

_____

_____

_____

_____

_____

_____

Just as in the water, face answers face,
so the heart of a person [speaks directly]
to [another] person.

—Proverbs 27:19

*T*he author of Proverbs, whom Jewish tradition considers to be Solomon, suggests to us that heartfelt words must be spoken face-to-face, unmasked, without filter or screen. There is no other way to do it. Greeting cards are insufficient. However, while we are mourning, others—even close friends and relatives—don't always know what to say to us. Some resort to clichés or truisms. They say things that they think we want to hear. Some avoid saying anything at all and avoid us entirely. So the tradition offers them guidance that we, too, must understand: Don't initiate conversation. Don't speak words to fill the quiet. Silence speaks more loudly than words when we speak in the language of the heart.

PERSONAL REFLECTIONS

_____

_____

_____

_____

_____

Tuesday/Yom Shelishi _____ (today's date)

I am a traveler on this earth. Do not hide your
mitzvot from me.

—Psalm 119:19

The Psalmist always offers us words to speak when we do not know how to compose the poetry of prayer. And in the Psalmist's words we find the idealized form of Jewish behavior, set apart from the secular Western world that is so familiar to us. Here, the Psalmist offers her simple plea to God—which echoes continuously in our hearts. We are freed from the obligation of most mitzvot during mourning because we may feel isolated and angry. So the tradition is cautious about keeping us in close proximity to God. But these mitzvot also connect us to our Maker. So we long for them, since we know that they help us rediscover and reaffirm that relationship.

PERSONAL REFLECTIONS

_____

_____

_____

_____

_____

_____

_____

*Rabbi Ezekiel of Kosmir, the Kosmirer Rebbe,
said to a disciple who had stopped his frequent
visits to him, "A person is like matzah dough.
When it is kneaded and rolled, it is fit to be eaten
as unleavened bread, but as soon as it is left
alone, it rises and becomes* hametz."

It is the same thing with people. In the modern world, we have made many choices about where to live. As certain neighborhoods disintegrated, often we moved away from local synagogues. Often we move from our hometowns, separating ourselves from parents and siblings. We feel this distance most acutely during the initial period of mourning as supportive family members return to their home communities and we do the same. In its wisdom, Jewish mourning tradition moves us back into community. It does not let us mourn alone. We mourn in the context of our community, where friends are transformed into family. And, as a result, following the counterintuitive inclination that Jewish spirituality often takes, the matzah dough, instead of rising and becoming buoyant, prepares us for the exodus from our isolation by prohibiting the rise and fermentation.

PERSONAL REFLECTIONS

_____

_____

> *The Gerer Rebbe taught that exile contains*
> *redemption within itself just as the seed contains*
> *the fruit. Right work and real diligence will bring*
> *out the hidden reward.*

It may be hard to understand the Gerer Rebbe's wisdom right now as we feel the intensity of exile in the midst of our mourning. The death of one we loved quickly disconnects us from the familiar world we once knew. As a result, we may feel as if we are facing this experience alone. But our ancestors faced similar challenges to their faith throughout their journey. They felt the realness of their exile throughout their desert wanderings. And eventually they reached the promised land of their redemption. That's where the Gerer Rebbe's wisdom is so instructive: Our personal redemption is a model for the ultimate redemption that will come. If we would only wait—and work—for it.

PERSONAL REFLECTIONS

_____

_____

_____

_____

_____

*While Moses was tending the flocks of his father-in-law
Jethro, the priest of Midian, he drove the flock into
the wilderness and came to Horeb, the mountain of
God. An angel of God appeared to him in a blazing fire
out of the bush. He gazed, and there was a bush all
aflame, yet the bush was not consumed.*

—Exodus 3:1–2

Isolated from others, Moses experienced the revelation
of the burning bush. We often write off this amazing encounter too quickly. Moses left the security of his home,
and in the midst of tending flocks, he came into contact
with God. Sometimes in the midst of our own soul's solitary journey, a moment when we may feel most isolated,
an experience of the Divine may be possible. That is often
how we feel during mourning—even when we are surrounded by family and friends and members of our community. In their midst, we may not always anticipate a
burning bush vision or a desert experience, but the presence of God that we can feel is no less real. So, as mourners and like Moses, we take off our shoes and prepare to
meet God.

PERSONAL REFLECTIONS

_____

_____

_____

When you call Me and come and pray to Me,
I will hear you. When You seek Me, you will find
Me. If you search for Me with all your heart,
I shall let you find Me.
—Jeremiah 29:12–14

*T*he prophet is God's spokesperson. Being a prophet may seem like a terrific job, but it was never easy for the prophet to do this work. As might be expected, people did not always want to hear the words contained in God's message. It was easier to pretend that the words were directed to someone else. Because people are often unwilling to listen, we read these prophetic words in public assembly on Shabbat following the reading of the Torah. The prophet's directions to us are quite clear. God has given us specific instructions concerning how we might find the holy and sacred in our midst. It is something that we need to hear throughout our lives, particularly as we weave our way through this maze of mourning. We do this so we can find our way to wholeness once again.

PERSONAL REFLECTIONS

_____

_____

_____

_____

A Meditation Before Saying Kaddish

❧

In March the snows do not last long. No sooner have they fallen than a rain falls and it is as if the snow had never been. Late one Friday evening I walked home through such a snow. I had the universe to myself and that unequaled joy of making the only footprints in the new snow. Occasionally, I turned around and walked backwards so I could watch the tracks that I had just created. Later that night, it warmed up and rained and by the time I returned to the synagogue the next morning there was not a trace of white to be found. But as I walked back retracing my steps it was as if the footprints remained. Perhaps there are traces people leave behind them in space and time as they make their way through the universe. Traces that cannot be eradicated. Through kings and wars and violence. Traces that tell all. Even though the snow has melted overnight.

—RABBI LAWRENCE KUSHNER,
INVISIBLE LINES OF CONNECTION

Resignation

Sunday/Yom Rishon ＿＿＿＿＿＿ (today's date)

Noah walked with God.

—Genesis 6:9

*T*his is a simple statement with profound consequences. It shapes nearly all that follows in the Bible and directs the lives of all of our biblical ancestors. Years before the desert journey and the Exodus, way before the covenant on Sinai was established with the Jewish people, and longer still before we have come to realize, in this modern era, that we are not "masters of our own universe," Noah established a model for behavior for humankind—even though he was far from perfect. While scholars have deduced specific elements of that Noachide model of behavior (as it has come to be called), one aspect is key: a relationship with God that forms the basis for our association with everyone else and with the world that surrounds us. Noah survived the flood. Likewise, with God at our side, we can indeed walk forward and find strength and solace to help us through our sorrow.

PERSONAL REFLECTIONS

Were it not for my delight in Your Torah, then in
my affliction, I would have felt that You were
lost to me.

—Psalm 119:92

*R*egardless of the reason, we can always turn to Torah. In one midrash, a rabbi suggests that our pursuit of Torah should be just like fish who rush to consume each raindrop falling into the ocean—thirsting for water though they are surrounded by it. The Torah process sometimes seems complicated. We can regularly find reasons to avoid Torah study. Because of our current experience of mourning, we may deny ourselves the uplifting pleasure of a relationship with God through an encounter with sacred text. In our pain, we may feel that God has become too distant from us, no longer involved in our daily lives. But this we must remember: Even in the darkest of times, we can see the Divine clearly through the reflected light of Torah.

PERSONAL REFLECTIONS

_____

_____

_____

_____

_____

Rabbi Yerachmiel of Przysucha taught: "A merchant is willing to undergo the hardships of travel in order to gain a livelihood. In the same way, we should be prepared to accept the hardships of this world with complete indifference in order to gain the fear of Heaven."

*W*e all have work to do and we need to continue to do it, despite what gets in our way. The "work" of mourning is arduous. While mourning, we learn that the most profound Torah can be found in the routine of daily living. Similarly, Rabbi Yerachmiel taught that we must understand what it takes to do our *jobs*. If we can accept the hurdles that we face in our routine work, which is filled with days of difficult choices, then we can move forward and succeed. This is possible when we are able to recognize that difficult work will lead to a greater good. Such an approach to our occupations lets us develop a similar approach to our real *work* in the world: Discovering where God can be found.

PERSONAL REFLECTIONS

_____

_____

_____

_____

Rabbi Moshe Leib of Sassov taught:
"If you cannot comprehend a mortal's thoughts,
how much less can you hope to comprehend
God's reasons. All that is possible is merely to
have faith."

As humans, we don't understand many things. We can try to hide behind the camouflage of knowledge and learning, but the truth remains of our persistent ignorance. As much as we try to understand the complexities of the universe through our personal experience with it, there is much about the world that will always elude us. It is all part of the human paradox. Likewise, there are those who believe that the more we try to understand the ways of God, the more distant the Divine Presence seems. Only when we let go of the struggle to know God is real understanding possible. For that, we need faith. But what is its source? A love of God that makes understanding possible; a love that reflects the hidden potential inherent only in a relationship with the Divine.

PERSONAL REFLECTIONS

_____

_____

_____

_____

A person is required to bless God for evil,
even as one is required to praise God for good.

—Babylonian Talmud, *Berakhot* 54a

*T*his is perhaps one of the most difficult mitzvot of all. It is one of the reasons why it is recorded explicitly in the Talmud. Our sacred literature teaches us about the entirety of our lives; it may even be considered a reflection of them. So our sacred texts resound with the reality of a world that is both good and bad, that is fair and unfair. Consequently, the texts force us to face things that we often want to avoid. This is a simple lesson with profound consequences: We have to find a way to accept the presence of both good and bad (even as we work to rid the world of evil), since unfortunately we cannot live in this world without one or the other. We have no choice, even as we try to change what we can, for to change death, we would also be forced to change life.

PERSONAL REFLECTIONS

_____

_____

_____

_____

_____

> *The more the Pharaoh afflicted them, the more*
> *they grew and filled the land.*
>
> —Exodus 1:12

This core Jewish idea is usually taught as part of the Passover story. And even if we know the story of Passover, we are obligated to tell it each year so that we might learn it again for ourselves and teach it to others. Egyptian slavery did not squelch the people's passion for living. According to Jewish tradition, it was only when the Israelites grew accustomed to slavery—after 400 years of living in Egypt—that God felt the urgent need to provide for their redemption. This Torah text presents us with a survival lesson from the folk history of the Jewish people. No matter how much pain and persecution we have been forced to endure, we have always found the strength to rise above it. And we always will.

PERSONAL REFLECTIONS

_____

_____

_____

_____

_____

_____

Saturday/Shabbat _____ (today's date)

The whole earth is at rest and untroubled; they
break forth in singing.

—Isaiah 14:7

Regardless of how we choose to enjoy the spirit of Shabbat, it is during this time that we have the freedom to do things that our hectic schedule has prevented us from doing the rest of the week. We are even freed from the demands of mourning and all that it implies. It seems strange, but for a short time (twenty-five hours according to the traditional reckoning of Shabbat time) we can return to that simpler time in Paradise that is completely like Shabbat. It is what the rabbis call *yom shekulo Shabbat* (literally, "a time that is fully Shabbat"). In the midst of it all, we can gain insights—as we learn from all those who struggle with us to find the way to help buoy our spirits and sustain us.

PERSONAL REFLECTIONS

_____

_____

_____

_____

_____

_____

A Meditation
Before Saying Kaddish

⟨∞⟩

*W*e can't pray that You make our lives free of problems; this won't happen and it is probably just as well. We can't ask You to make us and those we love immune to disease, because You can't do that. We can't ask You to weave a magic spell around us so that bad things will only happen to other people, and never to us. . . . But people who pray for courage, for strength to bear the unbearable, for the grace to remember what they have left instead of what they have lost, very often find their prayers answered. They discover that they have more strength, more courage than they ever knew themselves to have.

—*Adapted from* Rabbi Harold S. Kushner

Disengagement

Sunday/Yom Rishon _____ (today's date)

Noah was a righteous man, blameless in his age.
—Genesis 6:9

Our teachers wondered about these words from Genesis. The world is created dramatically, then things quickly deteriorate. If we accept that Noah was thoroughly righteous, then we are forced to deny what we learn about him after the Flood. We may consider his righteousness in the context of his time: The world had become so corrupt that God washed it clean with the Flood. Instead, we should address what we mean by "righteousness" in the same way that we do when we remember those we love who are no longer with us. They are righteous—and their lives are for a blessing—specifically because of all the good work they did despite the challenges of the human world in which they lived. May we continue their good work.

PERSONAL REFLECTIONS

_____

_____

_____

_____

_____

_____

*A certain caravan merchant said to Rabbah bar
Bar Channah, "Come, I will show you the place
where heaven and earth touch so closely that it
appears like they are kissing."*
—Babylonian Talmud, *Bava Batra* 74a

*T*hroughout my travels, I have looked for this place described by the Talmud. It always tops my travel itinerary. But I have been disappointed during each trip. Each time I have come close to what I concluded was *that* place, it always seemed to elude me. As we spiritually mature, we realize that we need not wander far away to find the place described by the caravan merchant. There is no need to venture halfway around the world to find it or to isolate ourselves from others to see that place more clearly. And that's what many of us do following the period of mourning. Then we come home to find that the place where heaven and earth touch is wherever we stand—if we are willing to lift up our eyes.

PERSONAL REFLECTIONS

_____

_____

_____

_____

_____

Tuesday/Yom Shelishi _____ (today's date)

> *Truth springs out of the earth.*
> —Psalm 85:12

One of the reasons we place clods of earth on a casket at the end of a funeral is to remind us of the ultimate reality of death. We are reminded of our own mortality and our inseparable connection to this physical world. It is the kind of ritual sound that leaves an indelible imprint on our memory. The soil's crunching sound incessantly echoes in our hearts. We try to silence it through the noise of the secular world as we start our normal routine again. But we should not try to silence it. That's its purpose. It helps us to understand what the Psalmist teaches in her wisdom, "Truth springs out of the earth," even as we humans are forced to eventually return to it.

PERSONAL REFLECTIONS

_____

_____

_____

_____

_____

_____

Pinchas of Koretz often prayed, "Adonai, lead me in the path of truth."

Why would the great Hasidic teacher Pinchas of Koretz, who was capable of weaving masterful paeans of praise, choose this modest prayer as his favorite? And why do we relate so strongly to his simple words? Pinchas knew that on the path of truth God could lead him anywhere he needed to go. This text from the Talmud summarizes the sentiment nicely for us: "My feet lead me to the place that I love" (Babylonian Talmud, *Sukkah* 53a). Like us, Pinchas knew in his heart that without Divine guidance he would continue to see merely what he wanted to see and would be unable to gain his bearings. Such limited vision would lead him away from the path of Divine truth—the path that he desperately sought to follow.

PERSONAL REFLECTIONS

_____

_____

_____

_____

_____

_____

> *Did God not know where Adam was?*
> *God asked [where Adam was] in order to open*
> *a way for [Adam to find to] repentance.*
> —*Tanchuma, Tazria* 1:9

*C*learly, God knew where Adam was hiding after he ate of the fruit of the tree of knowledge of good and evil. Adam arrogantly wanted to be like God. That's one reason he ate the fruit. Eventually, God called out to Adam, "*Ayekah:* Where are you?" But God always knows where we hide. By calling out to Adam, God offered him a way to find his own way back in the human world, which he had tried to leave behind. It's one of the many perspectives on repentance that the Torah offers us. Likewise, Rabbi Joseph Soloveitchik taught that "mourning is intrinsically an expression of repentance." We all need to find our own way back. God just wants to help clear the path for us.

PERSONAL REFLECTIONS

_____

_____

_____

_____

_____

_____

> *This is the sign that I have set as a covenant*
> *between you and Me. . . . I have set My rainbow*
> *in the clouds and it shall serve as a sign of that*
> *covenant between Me and the earth.*
>
> —Genesis 9:12–13

*F*or the Jewish people, creating memory is more important than recording history. In fact, Jewish history is the
collective memory of the Jewish people. That's why our
memory as Jews dates back to the creation of the world
as it is described early in the Book of Genesis. As we go
about our lives, we encounter subtle reminders of people
and events from our collective past. The memories are
often unfocused and fleeting. We may not even realize
that they have taken place until after they have occurred.
Sometimes the memory is triggered by a simple word, a
picture, or even a fragrance. This is particularly true as
we mourn for the one we loved and lost. So God rein-
forces our memory through the rainbow and reminds us
of the enduring nature of creation.

PERSONAL REFLECTIONS

_____

_____

_____

_____

_____

Saturday/Shabbat _____ (today's date)

> *To you who revere My Name, the sun*
> *of righteousness shall arise with healing*
> *on its wings.*
>
> —Malachi 3:20

*A*ccording to Jewish tradition, we can't measure time on Shabbat in the same way we calculate it during the rest of the week. On Shabbat, the days of Paradise are blended with the world-to-come, a time that is considered beyond time. It is a special day that arrives even before the early morning sun. During our days of bereavement, time takes on a different dimension as well. It is slow and heavy. It, too, is a time unlike all time. During this special Shabbat time—even in the midst of our mourning—we are provided with the opportunity to think about other things, the things that are really important and that eclipse everything else. In doing so, our world is sustained.

PERSONAL REFLECTIONS

_____

_____

_____

_____

_____

_____

A Meditation
Before Saying Kaddish

⟪∞⟫

Rebbe Nachman of Breslov taught, "This is the way to live the life of a true, pure Jew every single day of your life. No matter who you are, you can always find new vitality and strength through truth. The truth is God's own light—and there is no darkness in the world that is too dark for God. There is no impurity or unholiness in the world without exits to escape through. It is just that people don't see them because of the intense darkness there. Through the truth, however, God will shine to them and help them see the openings of hope that exist even in the lowest depths. This is the way to escape the darkness and go into the light and constantly come close to God."

—*LIKKUTEI MOHARAN* 1:112

Defiance

Sunday/Yom Rishon _____ (today's date)

> *Take note of the pattern that you will be shown*
> *on the mountain and make [the menorah]*
> *in like manner.*
>
> —Exodus 25:40

*T*his selection refers to instructions for building the ancient Tabernacle. Usually, we think that an artist is free to follow his or her own inclinations. But the Torah is telling us something else. As humans, certain limitations have been placed on the many things that we want to do. At the end of our lives, our work may yet be unfinished— and someone else has to take over those tasks. This is not easy, so we take our cues from the Divine. That's why the pattern for the menorah (remember: Light is a symbol of the Divine) was shown to the ancient Israelite artisans. Always take note of the pattern that God provides for us and try to imitate it. That is how we become holy—and how we make our lives holy as well.

PERSONAL REFLECTIONS

_____

_____

_____

_____

_____

> *God created in the human everything God*
> *created in the world. . . . Whatever God created*
> *in the universe, God fashioned [on a smaller*
> *scale] in humans.*
>
> —*Avot deRabbi Natan* 31:3

*W*e are replicas of the universe. Some suggest the opposite, claiming that the world is a projection of our human selves. Regardless, both are intimately connected. As we encounter the world—and slowly reengage it as we go through the stages of mourning—we are reminded of the natural patterns of life and living, of birth and maturation and the inevitability of decay. It is part of the harsh reality we must face; the earth provides us with evidence of this cycle of life wherever we go. It is perhaps one reason why we customarily cover mirrors during the initial stages of mourning and only uncover them as we venture out of our homes again. With the mirrors uncovered and mourning begun, we might be able to see the reflections of a world anew.

PERSONAL REFLECTIONS

_____

_____

_____

_____

The world is built on kindness.

—Psalm 89:3

The continued existence of the world depends on kindness. But such kindnesses are not random. This notion is affirmed in *Pirke Avot*, where we are taught: "The world stands on three things: Torah, prayer, and loving deeds of kindness" (1:2). We understand this sentiment more vividly during mourning than perhaps any other time. These acts of kindness fall into the category of what is called *chesed v'emet* (literally, *true* acts of kindness). During a crisis of leadership, as Moses stood at the shore of the Red Sea and lifted up his staff to separate the waters, several Israelites held up Moses' arms to support the weight of his burden. As we mourn, people extend themselves as well. And we are literally held up and supported by their deeds.

PERSONAL REFLECTIONS

_____

_____

_____

_____

_____

_____

Rabbi Nachman bar Yitzchak asks, "What is
written on the tefillin of the Master of the
Universe?" He replied, "And who is like Your
people Israel, a unique nation on earth?"
—Babylonian Talmud, *Berachot* 6a

*M*ost people have not given much consideration to
this talmudic excerpt, relegating it to rabbinic fantasy.
Does God—without body or form—strap on tefillin?
After all, the ritual of tefillin usually reminds us of our
devotion to God. So during this difficult time of mourning, we bind ourselves to God through the symbolism of
the tefillin. Now God is fearful that we may be lost to the
Divine through the process of our mourning. So God
straps the Divine tefillin on—struggling to hold us dear to
the Divine heart, so to speak. How do we know all this?
While our tefillin has God's name on it, according to this
passage from the Talmud, God's tefillin contains the
name of each Israelite, including our own.

PERSONAL REFLECTIONS

_____

_____

_____

_____

_____

If a person feels pain throughout his or her body,
let that individual engage in the study of Torah,
for she is called "a healing for the whole body"
(Proverbs 4:22).
———Babylonian Talmud, *Eruvin* 54a

*I*t is not Shabbat. It is only Thursday, the middle of the week, what we call "a Torah reading day." And that is the point of this talmudic lesson. We don't even have to wait for designated times to study. The study of our sacred texts is part of the mourning process. We study in order to honor the memory of the one who has died and to guide our own steps along the path of journey of our ancestors. We should dedicate our study to that person in public forum and in the privacy of our personal practices. Our devotion to that study while we are bereaved helps us understand that we study Torah to heal ourselves and to bring healing to those around us.

PERSONAL REFLECTIONS

_____

_____

_____

_____

_____

_____

You may not see my face. No human may see
My face and live.

—Exodus 33:20

*W*hat is it about casting our eyes on the Divine Presence that would rob us of the very breath of life that God gave us? Perhaps the ecstasy of such an encounter would be too much for us to bear. Or maybe were we able to look at God face-to-face (*panim el panim*, as the Torah calls it), we might mistakenly consider ourselves equals. Thus, we have to settle for different, more subtle kinds of experiences of God. Sometimes we can see God most clearly when we would least expect it, when God at first seems so far away. It is in the context of mourning that our acknowledgment of God's presence in our midst offers us life and restores our breath.

PERSONAL REFLECTIONS

_____

_____

_____

_____

_____

_____

_____

It is You alone, God. You made the heaven,
the most exalted heaven [the highest spiritual
spheres] and all their legions, the earth and
everything on it, the seas and everything in them,
and You gave them all life.

—Nehemiah 9:6

Nehemiah's words encourage us to enter into dialogue with the world, to take cognizance of God's miraculous creation even as events in our lives may cloud our vision. It's easier on Shabbat, when we are generally more attuned to blessing. So we pay attention to the things around us and offer a blessing. By using these words, they automatically bring us into relationship with the Divine—when we feel so isolated and distant from God. Whether it is the traditional formula for blessing identified by Jewish tradition (*Barukh atah Adonai* . . . , which I like to translate as "I thank You God for . . .") or just words that come to mind, hold the one that you mourn close to your heart. God will help transform whatever words we choose into prayer.

PERSONAL REFLECTIONS

_____

_____

_____

_____

A Meditation
Before Saying Kaddish

❦

*J*onathan spoke to David saying, "Your chair will be empty. You will be missed."

As our families gather around our dining room tables, whether welcoming the New Year, Passover, Thanksgiving, Hanukkah, or Shabbat, we often feel the presence of those who used to share our festival meals together. After a loss, Shabbat and the holidays are often times to realize that there is a chair at the family table that is empty.

Sitting at our dining tables, with the candles, china, silver, challah, wine, and good food, we can feel the spiritual presence of those who have sat with us in the past—those who have shared those meals, those who used to prepare the meals that we now prepare ourselves. Sitting in a sanctuary on Shabbat, Rosh Hashanah, Yom Kippur, or other holidays, we might well recall parents, grandparents, children, teachers, and family members who are no longer alive, yet their presence is felt. It is as if there were an empty chair or place next to us where they should be.

The chair is empty, but we know they continue to be seated among us. There is consolation and comfort to be found in the awareness that we continue to feel the presence of those who have influenced and touched our lives. Their teachings, advice, and wisdom did not die with them. They are still present to us and alive through us.

It is fitting to recall those who have most profoundly shaped us. They sit at our side. Their spirit is felt in our homes. They will always merit a place at our tables, for they have earned a place in our hearts. May we continue to be blessed with the gift of memory, and may we strive to live our lives in fulfillment of the noblest values and most sacred visions of those who have loved us and those whom we have loved.

—RABBI SAMUEL N. GORDON

TWO

The Disorganization of My Life

May the Holy One of Blessing comfort you among the other mourners for Zion and Jerusalem.
—Traditional words of comfort spoken to a mourner.

⟅∽∽∽⟆

*M*y grandmother used to speak a great deal about the *moloch hamaves,* the angel of death, as she merged Old World stories with an insightful, potently modern understanding of human suffering. And she lived through so much pain herself. This mythic angel reflected real experience and frequently hovered over our family in my childhood and in my adult life, constantly threatening those we loved, even though we tried desperately to keep it at bay. And whenever it struck, our lives were thrown into disarray and the familiar, routine measurement of time lost its meaning. Nights and days often fused together in an undifferentiated blur. Only the mourning process had any relevance or meaning. This kind of chaos occurs even when death is expected, anticipated, even welcomed, after a long illness or a hospital stay.

Jewish tradition tells us to stop everything that we are doing, acknowledge God, rend our garments, and immediately start the mourning process so we can find our mooring and stability when we need it most. As soon as a loved one dies, the details of our daily lives become essentially irrelevant and lose their importance. It is the process of mourning, the result of the evolution of Jewish ritual over time that helps us reorganize our lives and establish a new rhythm for daily living.

The Torah tells us that the world was *tohu vavohu* ("dark and in disarray") prior to God's work of creation. Then "God's spirit hovered over the earth" and brought order out of the chaos. Set into motion, the world followed a certain order or set pattern (what the rabbis call *olam kenegdo*), something that we come to expect, something on which we depend. But just as this order is never like it was at Creation, our lives really never again return to the way they once were. This sense of disarray and disorder lies under the surface of even what appears to be orderly. And we are forced to find our way through it—guided by God and by Jewish tradition.

Turmoil

Lekh lekha. *Get yourself out of your country,
from among your kin.*

—Genesis 12:1

With familiar words, God sent Abraham forward to
continue his journey. It was uncomfortable for him to
leave behind all that he knew. As might be expected, he
hesitated, unwilling to go forward. We may not always
hear the call as clearly as did Abraham, but we are often
similarly motivated to move on. Something happens in
our lives, something that is not always pleasant. But it
forces us to move to places when we may not have anticipated any move at all. And we learn that we can never really return to the place from whence we came. But before
we can set our lives back in order, we must ask ourselves
two questions: How did we get here? What made us
make this stop along the way?

PERSONAL REFLECTIONS

_____

_____

_____

_____

_____

_____

*Never miss the opportunity to study the word of
God. It settles the mind and calms the heart.*
—Rebbe Nachman of Breslov

*S*tudy is part of the routine of Jewish living. Just as it helps shape our lives, it also shapes our mourning. So we study just a little each day. Most people think that we study in order to learn more about sacred text or to acquire an intellectual accumulation of facts and figures. Some people even believe that our quest for Jewish knowledge is now motivated by the need in this electronic age for instant, nearly limitless information. But sacred study teaches us about the slow development of an ongoing relationship with the Divine. This is especially important now that we need it most. Study is a form of prayer. To reap its benefits, we have to slow down—and bring order back into our world.

PERSONAL REFLECTIONS

_____

_____

_____

_____

_____

_____

> *Rava said: "A person is not held responsible for*
> *what he [or she] says in an hour of distress."*
> —Babylonian Talmud, *Bava Batra* 16b

*A*t certain times in our lives, particularly when we are mourning, we may say things—to others, to ourselves, and particularly to God—that we will later regret. Jewish tradition understands the plight of the mourner. While no one can fully comprehend the depth of our pain, the rabbis do grasp its severity. Instead of pretending to be able to remove the heart's ache—which no human can do—the sages offer insight and understanding as we attempt to comprehend the basic paradox of human life. But Rava's statement removes the obligation for future action to remedy the harm done by our words. It helps set the soul free at a time when it is burdened with grief.

PERSONAL REFLECTIONS

_____

_____

_____

_____

_____

_____

_____

_____

By the waters of Babylon, there we sat down and
wept when we remembered Zion.

—Psalm 137:1

*T*hese are the words of exile, first spoken by our ancestors after they were forced to leave their homes in the
Promised Land and live in Babylonia. The ancient Temple
had been destroyed, and Jerusalem was converted to rubble. Understandably, the people longed to return to life as
it once was. For them and for us, the past always seems
better than the present. But the future is ours to fashion.
Later this statement became the standard cry of Jews
who, anywhere and anytime, kept the dream of Israel as a
fire burning in their hearts. The memory of that first
exile, the memory of the Jewish people, merges with our
personal exile, cast out, as we are now, from the presence
and the support of a loved one. Time and time again, our
people rose from the ashes of destruction. We will do the
same.

PERSONAL REFLECTIONS

_____

_____

_____

_____

_____

My heart is in the East, and I am in the West.
—Yehuda Halevi

These words, originally written by a great medieval poet, reflect a Jewish sentiment that has buoyed us throughout our history. Regardless of the wars that ravaged Jerusalem or were fought to diminish it, this holy city remains the spiritual center of the Jewish world. The Psalmist understood it clearly when she wrote: "If I forget thee, O Jerusalem, let my right hand wither and let my tongue cleave to the roof of my mouth" (Psalm 137:5–6). Wherever we have lived, whether in exile or in freedom, Jerusalem has enriched the Jewish heart. Regardless of where we are, we turn toward it in prayer. Even when we are unsure of our own direction in life, we are instructed to turn our hearts toward Jerusalem, for that is our constant, reassuring, and eternal beacon.

PERSONAL REFLECTIONS

_____

_____

_____

_____

_____

_____

Friday/Yom Shishi _____ (today's date)

> *Hear O Israel, Adonai is our God,*
> *Adonai is One.*
>
> —Deuteronomy 6:4

*I*n Jewish tradition, this statement, which is called the *Shema* (literally, "hear" or "pay attention"), is said twice daily during formal worship. It also forms the core of those prayers said before retiring at night (the "*shema al hamitah*"). Similarly, we are instructed to say the *Shema* as our last words as we approach death. The *Shema* is as close as Judaism comes to a statement of creed, for it is the foundation on which all of Judaism is built. So we place it in the mezuzah that is affixed to the doorposts of our homes and in the tefillin that we bind to ourselves each morning. We look for opportunities to remind ourselves of one certainty in the midst of all that is uncertain: God is One.

PERSONAL REFLECTIONS

_____

_____

_____

_____

_____

_____

Saturday/Shabbat _____ (today's date)

*Keep faith with Adonai your God, walking in
God's ways, carrying out the laws, mitzvot, rules
of justice and directions of God, as written in the
Torah of Moses, so that you may succeed in all
that you do and whatever you turn to.*

—1 Kings 2:3

*K*ing David is remembered for many things during his forty-year reign, including drawing Israel and Judea into a united kingdom. Prior to his death, he offered the above words to his son, Solomon, who would soon be king. David wanted to tell Solomon many things. Through his actions, including many misdeeds, David had learned a great deal about God. Although David often strayed from a righteous path, he returned and developed an intimate relationship with God. According to Jewish tradition, the Messiah will come from the lineage of David. Like so many of us, he was at first not prepared to learn some of these lessons. But here is the main lesson he clearly wanted to pass on to his son: Follow God and your path will be made clear.

PERSONAL REFLECTIONS

_____

_____

_____

_____

A Meditation
Before Saying Kaddish

⟨∞⟩

Not to mourn is to disrespect the deceased; to mourn excessively is not to accept God's own bereavement over God's action. Not to mourn is to trivialize the sanctity of life, to mourn overmuch is to betray future life.

Agnon [a modern Hebrew essayist] suggested that the mourner's Kaddish, which sanctifies and magnifies God's name, is meant to comfort God. For indeed, if we are created in God's image, our death is God's diminution. How do we praise God's name? An anonymous commentator translates a verse in Psalms, "Adonai is my shadow," with a parable. The shadow is our reflection. If we walk stooped over, the shadow grows smaller—but if we walk erect, the shadow is lengthened. Kaddish is recited not when we are seated and not when we are alone, but when we are on our own two feet and in the presence of community. Rising in the face of adversity, we raise divinity. In so doing, we raise our own spirits.

—*Adapted from* RABBI HAROLD M. SCHULWEIS

Chaos

Sunday/Yom Rishon _____ (today's date)

Let your brother live beside you.
—Leviticus 25:36

This seems like a strange statement for the Torah, particularly in the midst of the Book of Leviticus (which is often referred to as *Torat Kohanim,* the Book of the Priests, since its rules and regulations are designed to lead individuals to the purity of the priesthood). Often, mourning and bereavement force families together in ways that have not been done since childhood. We see it happening throughout the Torah, particularly in the reunion of Jacob and Esau at their father's burial site. The reconfiguration of relationships in the midst of mourning can be difficult for some families. So after all of your friends and some of your relatives have returned to their regular routine and you are still trying to put your life back in order, remember to "let your brother live beside you."

PERSONAL REFLECTIONS

_____

_____

_____

_____

_____

_____

Monday/Yom Sheni _____ (today's date)

> *Happy is the one whose ancestors transmit merit*
> *to him. Happy is the one who has a noble family*
> *tree on which to hold fast.*
> —Jerusalem Talmud, *Berakhot* 4:1, 7d

*T*his relationship between the generations of the past and present is something that we have come to expect. But we are more than the sum total of our past. Jewish tradition teaches that we have the ability, through our actions, to transform the misdeeds of those who have come before us, even those of our parents. According to tradition, Abraham's father was a maker of idols. After hearing God's call, Abraham rejected the idolatry of his father and smashed his father's idols before fashioning a faith of his own for us to share. Abraham's faith brought merit to his father. Such transformation of faith is something that we can all do—and sometimes something that we must do.

PERSONAL REFLECTIONS

_____

_____

_____

_____

_____

_____

I lift my eyes to the hills:
Whence will my help come?
My help is from Adonai,
Maker of heaven and earth.

—Psalm 121:1, 2

*W*henever we read in the Bible that someone has "lifted one's eyes," we know that something significant is about to happen (what I like to call "Bible-speak"). When Joseph saw his brother Benjamin, we suspected the rapprochement that followed because Joseph "lifted his eyes" and saw his brothers in a way he had not previously experienced. Psalm 121 is read frequently during funerals. It has a gentle, captivating way of guiding mourners while lifting them at the same time. The Psalmist's words may also provide you with comfort while you are bringing order back to your world. This psalm helps us not because of the poetry of its words, but rather because of the direction in which the words take you: to God, Maker of heaven and earth.

PERSONAL REFLECTIONS

_____

_____

_____

_____

_____

*Every assembly that is for the sake of Heaven
must in the end abide.*

—*Pirke Avot* 4:11

*T*his is one of the many important sayings that makes *Pirke Avot* (a section of the Mishnah) such a unique source of the sages' guiding wisdom for everyday living. Traditionally, *Pirke Avot* is studied on Shabbat afternoon, particularly between Passover and Shavuot while we are anticipating the revelation of Torah. Consider the many groups of people that came together to support you in your mourning from the very moment that you learned that a loved one had died. Perhaps the most important of these is the daily minyan (the prayer quorum) that assembles for one reason alone: in order for you to say Kaddish each day in the midst of community. There are no intermediaries between you and God. Because their task is so important, these individual daily minyan groups are cared for personally by God.

PERSONAL REFLECTIONS

_____

_____

_____

_____

_____

Thursday/Yom Chamishi _____ (today's date)

*A generation goes and a generation comes, but
the earth stands forever.*
—Ecclesiastes 1:4

As we grow older, many of us feel that time seems to pass more rapidly. It is an intriguing phenomenon with no real scientific explanation. Perhaps it is because each year represents a smaller percentage of our lives. Or maybe it is because we have more obligations. Whatever the case, the words of Ecclesiastes (*Kohelet* in Hebrew) offer us a spiritual truth that cannot be measured by the exactitude of science. It is true that we all come and go. But we can be assured that the earth will abide even when we do not—and that someone else will continue our work. It is part of the *shalshelet hakabbalah* (the chain of tradition that links the generations) that with our lives we help to forge.

PERSONAL REFLECTIONS

_____

_____

_____

_____

_____

_____

Friday/Yom Shishi _____ (today's date)

> *Blessed shall you be when you enter and blessed*
> *shall you be when you depart.*
> —Deuteronomy 28:6

These words may be familiar to you as words of blessing offered whenever Jews gather to celebrate, commemorate, or mourn. They are particularly poignant on Shabbat, when tradition suggests that a pair of angels accompanies each individual on his or her way home from synagogue. Then these angels stay with us for the entire twenty-five-hour period of Shabbat. This notion is reflected in "Shalom Aleichem," a song that is sung at the Shabbat dinner table. As the sun slowly sets and casts its shadow upon us, we invite these angels to welcome us peacefully at the onset of Shabbat and to leave us in peace when they depart during *Havdalah*, the conclusion of Shabbat. And may they protect us in our present fragility during the week ahead.

PERSONAL REFLECTIONS

_____

_____

_____

_____

_____

_____

> *I, the Eternal, have been your God*
> *Ever since the land of Egypt;*
> *You have known no [real] God but Me,*
> *There is no Redeemer besides Me.*
>
> —Hosea 13:4

*T*he experience in Egypt helped form us as a people. It is, therefore, part of the collective memory of the Jewish people that we have carried through history. Unlike Moses, who had already established a relationship with God, most of the Israelites developed their relationship with God during the wilderness journey from Egypt to Canaan, beginning with their exodus from slavery. Whether it was the Divine cloud or God's pillar of fire that helped lead them on their way, they certainly felt the Divine Presence. Nevertheless, it was not an easy journey for them. And not all of them made it. Spiritual journeys of this sort are generally not easy, but they are often transformative. Likewise, in the adversity of our mourning and our slow travel from chaos to order, we may get to know God in ways we previously never thought possible.

PERSONAL REFLECTIONS

_____

_____

_____

_____

A Meditation
Before Saying Kaddish

⟨∽∿∽⟩

The past has become history and the future is uncertain, its veil unpenetrable.

A Hasidic tale bids us to dispel such a gloom. It tells of a woman from Kotzk who approached her rebbe, the great Menachem Mendl, and told him of her ceaseless pain. She had suffered a crushing loss some years before and was unable to pick up the shattered pieces of her life. "I am lost," she cried. "I can't function anymore. My life has turned into a never-ending darkness." And the Kotzker Rebbe replied, "What you do not realize is that whenever one gate of life closes, God makes sure to open another."

The Kotzker's counsel was wise. No purpose is served in rattling closed gates and bemoaning the past. We cannot rewind the clock of our lives to an earlier time. Far better to walk through those newly opened gates!

Indeed, on our own journey through life we encounter countless gates, and when one of them closes we must enter another or perish. We begin our independent lives only once when we emerge from the womb and lose its protective shelter. Later on, we leave our mothers and fathers and our child-hood homes. We become adults only when we forgo the pipe dreams of our childhood years and recog-nize that life will not permit us to realize them. We get married and have children and ultimately must let them go. We confront the death of our parents, our spouses, our friends, sometimes even our chil-dren, and somehow we must build life anew. We face the gradual or not so gradual waning of our own strength, and still we must forge ahead.

Life is never just "being." It is always a "becom-ing," a relentless flowing on. We move through the various stages of life, as Shakespeare put it, each with its entrances and exits—the infant becomes the child, the child becomes the adult—and there simply is no turning back.

—*Adapted from* RABBI ALEXANDER M. SCHINDLER

Confusion

Sunday/Yom Rishon _____ (today's date)

I have set before you life and death, blessing and curse. Therefore, choose life so that you and your offspring may live.

—Deuteronomy 30:19

*T*his is a puzzling statement for the Torah, even if it does come from God. It doesn't seem like much of a choice. Yet, regardless of our circumstances, opportunities in life abound. What we make of those opportunities and where we choose to go is totally up to us. But we can't always wait for opportunities to present themselves. Instead, we have to seize them and take control of our lives. This is particularly apt during the months of mourning when we sometimes feel that we have been robbed of our options in life as a result of the death of the one we love. But the choice to continue living remains ours.

PERSONAL REFLECTIONS

_____

_____

_____

_____

_____

_____

Where could I go from Your spirit?
Or where could I flee from Your presence?
If I climb to heaven, You are there,
there too, if I lie in the depths.

—Psalm 139:7–8

*B*ecause it reflects human experience, the Bible is full of people who tried to run from God or perhaps felt abandoned by the Divine Presence. There were even prophets—like Jonah—who tried to avoid the Divine call and their prophetic mission. Others were simple folk who traversed the desert feeling like they were going it alone even when they were surrounded by the 600,000 Israelites who were making the journey with them. Whenever we bear spiritual burdens, we feel alone in doing so. But the Psalmist's simple statement of faith is poignantly clear in its instruction to us. And it helps us to create some semblance of order during mourning. Wherever we go, whatever we experience, God will be there.

PERSONAL REFLECTIONS

_____

_____

_____

_____

_____

Tuesday/Yom Sheni _____ (today's date)

> *The one who learns for the purpose of teaching*
> *gains inspiration.*
> —*Leviticus Rabbah 35:7*

As Jews, regardless of our age or our level of literacy, we are obligated to study. It is part of what uniquely shapes us as a people. Study can steer us into a relationship with God. Since we generally do not study alone, study also brings us into a close alliance with another human being, our *chevruta* (study partner). Only during certain periods of time—including some of the early days of mourning—are we free to refrain from Torah study because it is a joy to study Torah. But we may study Lamentations and Job. We are never restricted from learning. Often, as we learn in mourning, instruction emerges from life's circumstances, and these transcend the written lesson.

PERSONAL REFLECTIONS

_____

_____

_____

_____

_____

_____

*Every drop that goes forth from Paradise carries
with it a drop of wisdom.*
—*Zohar* I, 125a

*B*ecause they stand on their own, some texts need little explanation. They require only vision. In the case of this selection from the *Zohar*, the primary mystical text in Jewish tradition, the vision can take us from the Paradise where Adam and Eve innocently frolicked, then we traverse history and the insights we have learned from it, and then apply it to the Messianic time which is beyond history. We get glimpses of both forms of Paradise on Shabbat. Like Sabbath moments we carry into the week, these glimpses help bring order back to our lives. We include the text on Wednesday because certain Jewish tradition suggests that we can keep Shabbat until Wednesday. Then we make *Havdalah* so we can prepare for Shabbat—and for our renewed vision of Paradise—once again.

PERSONAL REFLECTIONS

⎯⎯⎯⎯⎯⎯⎯⎯⎯⎯⎯⎯⎯⎯⎯⎯⎯⎯⎯⎯⎯⎯⎯⎯

⎯⎯⎯⎯⎯⎯⎯⎯⎯⎯⎯⎯⎯⎯⎯⎯⎯⎯⎯⎯⎯⎯⎯⎯

⎯⎯⎯⎯⎯⎯⎯⎯⎯⎯⎯⎯⎯⎯⎯⎯⎯⎯⎯⎯⎯⎯⎯⎯

⎯⎯⎯⎯⎯⎯⎯⎯⎯⎯⎯⎯⎯⎯⎯⎯⎯⎯⎯⎯⎯⎯⎯⎯

⎯⎯⎯⎯⎯⎯⎯⎯⎯⎯⎯⎯⎯⎯⎯⎯⎯⎯⎯⎯⎯⎯⎯⎯

⎯⎯⎯⎯⎯⎯⎯⎯⎯⎯⎯⎯⎯⎯⎯⎯⎯⎯⎯⎯⎯⎯⎯⎯

*One who stands in darkness can perceive what is
in light; But one who stands only in light cannot
pierce the surrounding darkness.*
—Rabbi Rami Shapiro

*U*sually we think of wisdom as issuing only from the past. We assign insight to ancient sages, while often forgetting that rabbis of our day have faced—and overcome—some of greatest spiritual challenges of the century. This is particularly true of today's generation of spiritual seekers who were raised on the messianic potential inherent in rational faith and scientific exactitude. But Rabbi Shapiro understands the darkness of mourning, as well as the brilliant light that is emitted by a questioning faith in a way that is perhaps unmatched by those who came before us. We have to stand resolutely in the dark in order to benefit from the light.

PERSONAL REFLECTIONS

_____

_____

_____

_____

_____

_____

Friday/Yom Shishi _____ (today's date)

Abraham rose early in the morning.
—Genesis 22:3

*A*braham's actions in this line from Genesis do not seem so special. It is not unusual for many of us to get up early in the morning. Some can't sleep. Others have early morning work schedules. But the Torah wants to teach us something more, and this is the Bible's peculiar way of writing within the lines. Abraham got up early to do something important. It is reflected in the traditional notion that one rises early to do a *mitzvah*. Abraham heard God's call—and responded to it. That is something we can all do, whenever we hear the word of God: Get up early and act. While mourning, don't lose faith in God. The future faith of Israel may depend on it.

PERSONAL REFLECTIONS

_____

_____

_____

_____

_____

_____

_____

You alone have I known
Of all the families of the earth.

—Amos 3:2a

*J*ewish tradition calls the people of Israel the chosen people because of the special relationship that God maintains with them. It all began with the giving of Torah on Mount Sinai. However, most Jews today are more comfortable with the notion of a "choosing people," since the Israelites chose to accept the Torah when it was presented to them after leaving Egypt. Like most relationships, the covenant between God and Israel places demands on both parties. The nature of that relationship is best manifest in the observance of *mitzvot*, those Divine instructions that have the potential to make each member of the people of Israel holy and chosen. Through those mitzvot, people come to know God as they come to know themselves. Both of these are particularly important in the midst of mourning.

PERSONAL REFLECTIONS

_____

_____

_____

_____

_____

A Meditation Before Saying Kaddish

〜

I often feel that death is not the enemy of life, but its friend, for it is the knowledge that our years are limited which makes them so precious. It is the truth that time is but lent to us which makes us, at our best, look upon our years as a trust handed into our temporary keeping. We are like children privileged to spend a day in a great park, a park filled with many gardens and playgrounds and azure-tinted lakes with white boats sailing upon the tranquil waves. True, the day allotted to each one of us is not the same in length, in light, in beauty. Some children of earth are privileged to spend a long and sunlit day in the garden of the earth. For others the day is shorter, cloudier, and dusk descends more quickly as in a winter's tale. But whether our life is a long summery day or a shorter wintry afternoon, we know that inevitably there are storms and squalls which overcast even the bluest heavens and there are sunlit rays which pierce the darkest autumn sky.

The day that we are privileged to spend in the great park of life is not the same for all human beings, but there is enough beauty and joy and gaiety in the hours if we will treasure them. Then for each one of us the moment comes when the great nurse, death, takes man, the child, by the hand and quietly says, "It is time to go home. Night is coming. It is your bedtime, child of earth. Come; you're tired. Lie down at last in the quiet nursery of nature and sleep. Sleep well. The day is gone. Stars shine in the canopy of eternity."

—*Adapted from* JOSHUA LOTH LIEBMAN

Bewilderment

> *[Pharaoh's says,] Come let us deal craftily with*
> *him [the Israelites].*
>
> —Exodus 1:10

*F*or the Israelites, the descent into slavery was rapid. With these several words spoken by a Pharaoh "who knew not Joseph"—nor cared about the good that he had done for Egypt—the Israelites were forced (some say tricked) into slavery. Eventually, God reached out to them "with a mighty arm and an outstretched hand" and delivered them to freedom through the leadership of Moses. As the story of their deliverance progresses, we learn that through Pharaoh's trickery, he outsmarted himself. No human, however powerful, is a match for the Divine. As we mourn, we pray for understanding. Like the Israelites in Egypt, God will redeem us from the slavery of our bewilderment.

PERSONAL REFLECTIONS

_____

_____

_____

_____

_____

_____

Monday/Yom Sheni _____ (today's date)

> *The path of the righteous is like the light at*
> *dawn, that shines more and more [until it is*
> *transformed] into the perfect day.*
>
> —Proverbs 4:18

*T*he work of the righteous lights the way for all of us as we move toward a more perfect world that eventually leads us to messianic time. According to Jewish tradition, thirty-six righteous persons in each generation sustain the world. Their work alone sustains us. We call them *lamed-vavniks*, using the Hebrew alphanumeric (of *lamed* and *vav*) for thirty-six. With the death of the one you mourn, one of the pillars of your world has been shattered. But the good works they performed do not have to cease. We can extend their acts of goodness by continuing something that they started. By doing so, we help to make their memory a blessing.

PERSONAL REFLECTIONS

_____

_____

_____

_____

_____

_____

Though it tarry, wait for it.

—Habakkuk 2:3

*L*ike most of the prophets, Habakkuk, the author of a three-chapter Biblical outcry over the ascent of the Chaldeans in the ancient Near East, spoke of the immediate future facing Israel, as well as the messianic future. This attitude of unyielding hope has inspired Jews throughout history. As a result, the Jewish people has come to understand the value of enduring patience. Regardless of where our travels have taken us, no matter where we have been forced (or chosen) to go, there we have waited for the Messiah, even here amid the limitless freedom of North America. Each Jewish worship service includes a fervent plea for a perfect future. The vision of such a future fosters the kind of hope that is indispensable during these gloomy periods in our lives. While we mourn, we also continue to wait.

PERSONAL REFLECTIONS

_____

_____

_____

_____

_____

_____

Wednesday/Yom Revii ＿＿＿＿＿ (today's date)

*Serve Adonai with reverential fear
and rejoice with trembling.*

—Psalm 2:11

*T*his has always been a difficult text for me to understand—and an even more difficult posture to achieve. This is particularly true during trying periods in my life, such as mourning, that really challenge the basic foundation of my faith. But the powerful lesson of the sacred text helps bring me closer to God rather than push me away from the Divine. In this text, the Psalmist encourages us to develop an intimate relationship with God, which may only be possible during such difficult times. So she also warns us of the inherent risks in fostering such a relationship. We have once again learned about the power of the Divine. Now we are instructed to rejoice in its intensity, ever mindful of its guiding influence in our lives.

PERSONAL REFLECTIONS

＿＿＿＿＿＿＿＿＿＿＿＿＿＿＿＿＿＿＿＿＿＿＿＿＿

＿＿＿＿＿＿＿＿＿＿＿＿＿＿＿＿＿＿＿＿＿＿＿＿＿

＿＿＿＿＿＿＿＿＿＿＿＿＿＿＿＿＿＿＿＿＿＿＿＿＿

＿＿＿＿＿＿＿＿＿＿＿＿＿＿＿＿＿＿＿＿＿＿＿＿＿

＿＿＿＿＿＿＿＿＿＿＿＿＿＿＿＿＿＿＿＿＿＿＿＿＿

＿＿＿＿＿＿＿＿＿＿＿＿＿＿＿＿＿＿＿＿＿＿＿＿＿

*The appointed seasons were given to Israel for
no other purpose than for them to enjoy
themselves. The Holy One said: If you enjoy
yourselves [this year], you will do so the
following year.*

—*Tanchuma, Bereishit* 4

The holiday calendar is a rich tapestry of Jewish life. We move from the majesty of Rosh Hashanah to the intensive introspection of Yom Kippur. The frivolity of Purim takes us to the contemplation of the serious questions during Passover of slavery and freedom. And then four weeks later, revelation takes place on Shavuot. The Jewish holiday cycle reflects the wide range of human emotions and the journey of the Jewish people as it explored its relationship with God. Each time we observe a holiday or celebration, we reflect on the observances of our ancestors. Through their eyes and ours, we can better understand the spiritual life of the Jewish soul. And this provides us with reason and order for our lives.

PERSONAL REFLECTIONS

_____

_____

_____

_____

> *A certain man found him [Joseph] and, behold,*
> *he was wandering in the field. So the man asked*
> *him, "What are you seeking?"*
> —Genesis 37:15

*J*oseph was confused before he met the stranger who directed him to his brothers in Dotan. Perhaps it was an innocent question, a friendly inquiry to someone who was obviously lost. Maybe the stranger was a Divine messenger or the Torah's way of reflecting Joseph's spiritual struggle with himself. In this short dialogue with a stranger—about which the Torah tells us very little—Joseph's destiny (and the future of Israel in Egypt) is determined. It is one of the most critical points in the Joseph story. When we are most confused, it seems that it is a stranger who points the way. He or she may be the one who helps you find your way—back to your essential self, the part that may have become eclipsed by mourning.

PERSONAL REFLECTIONS

_____

_____

_____

_____

_____

_____

> *Therefore [teach them]:*
> *one command and then another,*
> *one line and then another,*
> *a little here, a little there!*
>
> —Isaiah 28:10

*T*he rabbis teach us in *Pirke Avot* that we should honor whoever teaches us a verse, a sentence, a word, or even a letter of Torah. Elsewhere, we are taught that we should always recognize the teacher who taught us what it is that we are teaching in public. Sacred study is precious to the Jewish people. It is indispensable. But the teacher of these texts is even more precious. The prophet Isaiah understands the power of the words of sacred texts, for each verse is spoken on behalf of God. Through studying and understanding the Divine word, we may come to know God. Thus, during mourning, we continue to study—or begin afresh. Such study, particularly on Shabbat, brings us back—or forward—to Paradise.

PERSONAL REFLECTIONS

_____

_____

_____

_____

_____

A Meditation
Before Saying Kaddish

━━━━━━━━━━ ๑๑๑๑๑ ━━━━━━━━━━

Time alone cannot heal our sorrow and can even make it progress to a deeper estrangement. Time heals only if we have reached the stage of convalescence, and reaching that stage requires surgery—an opening up, a radical excision. Then, slowly and gently, the body-soul knits together the torn fiber of being. We experience two distinct pains, one physical and the other, more threatening, metaphysical. The second of these takes the form of the question, "What does this mean?" If we choose to suppress the second pain and dull or ignore the first, then time will increase the distress. However troubling it may be, we must see the pain as a gift, and we ignore it at great risk. So we must feel both kinds of pain fully, enter into the question boldly, and struggle with it tenaciously. The question cannot be answered on the cognitive level ("I know that loss is part of the human condition; it is not a sign that God no longer cares for me") any more than a malignancy can be excised cognitively. Our perception of God's Presence and caring engagement is visceral.

In our mourning we must first define the questions, always preceding at a deliberate pace. Then we will be ready to receive the answers that will come not as words but as experience—as a living stream that makes the wait healing.

—*Adapted from* CAROL OCHS

THREE

Directing My Anger

I am weary with groaning;
. . . I melt my couch in tears.
—Psalm 6:7

⌖

*A*nger, which can wreak havoc with our emotional and spiritual lives, is presumed by the mourning process in Judaism. When someone we love dies—always too young and never at the right time—we are angry. We are mad at God for not sparing this particular life, for creating a world that allows for death. Even when we are finally prepared to accept the death of another, because we have no choice but to do so, we may remain angry at God. As our tradition suggested when Abraham argued with God over the fate of the cities of Sodom and Gomorrah, we demand justice from a God of justice.

We are also angry at ourselves for not spending enough time with the person, for perhaps not saying all that we wanted to say to them while we still had the chance to say it. Our anger may affect all that we do, and we may express it in our relationships with others, even with those who are doing their best to try to make us feel better. But we may not want to feel better since, in a peculiar way, the pain keeps us connected to the one we have lost.

The challenge to this anger comes as our tradition guides us back to our routine life. But there can no longer be the same routine to our lives. Too many things have changed. So our task now is to find ways to direct that anger, to affirm our love for the deceased, and to sustain our memory of them.

Fury

Sunday/Yom Rishon _____ (today's date)

Adonai, Adonai, a God compassionate
and gracious, slow to anger,
rich in steadfast kindness.

—Exodus 34:6

This is the beginning of a list of descriptions from which Jewish tradition derives the thirteen basic attributes of God. While these items are repeated in various places in the liturgy, we hear the plaintive echo of its plea most frequently during the High Holidays as we stand before God in anticipation of judgment. That's why the words are sung during High Holiday services in a way that transforms this Torah text into a petition for God to accept our prayers with compassion and kindness and as an affirmation of our very belief in God. If we are to imitate God and become a holy nation, as the Torah advises, then we, too, must be compassionate and gracious, slow to anger, and extremely kind. And that is not easy at a time like this.

PERSONAL REFLECTIONS

_____

_____

_____

_____

_____

> *Speaking in the name of Rabbi Meir, Rav said,*
> *"When addressing the Holy Blessed One, one's*
> *words should be few, for Scripture says, 'Be not*
> *rash with your mouth . . . to utter a word before*
> *God. . . . ' (Ecclesiastes 5:1)."*
> —Babylonian Talmud, *Berakhot* 61a

*T*he assumption that we can only offer praise or petition before God shapes much of our formal liturgy. But our sages recognized that other things require expression and that there is room for anger in our relationship with God. One friend of mine—who attends worship services often—sits in synagogue and says nothing. When I questioned him about his lack of participation, he told me, "This is my individual form of protest to God." In whatever form it takes, this tradition of arguing before God (and expressing our displeasure) is called *chutzpah clappei malah* (literally, "arrogance in the face of [God] above"). Levi Yitzchak of Berditchev is best remembered for maintaining this posture throughout his life. Take whatever you have to God, but remember one thing: "When you pray, know before whom you stand" (Babylonian Talmud, *Berakhot* 28b).

PERSONAL REFLECTIONS

_____

_____

*No one except the Holy One can satisfy the wish
of every human being.*
—*Esther Rabbah* 2:14

*S*everal months have already passed since the funeral. Friends and relatives have returned to the regular rhythm of their lives. In a bit of convenient, but well-intentioned concern, every once in a while someone will ask how you are doing or if they can do anything for you. Politely, you may reply, "I'm fine." And yet, you are not fine. You still seethe with anger. No one seems able to say or do anything to help the anger abate. Their words may even increase your rage. No one understands your mourning, except God, Who feels your pain and can comfort you. When God seems distant, it is because we have left no room in our lives for the Divine. So open yourself to God and be comforted.

PERSONAL REFLECTIONS

_____

_____

_____

_____

_____

_____

Wednesday/Yom Revii _____ (today's date)

> *Speaking in the name of Rabbi Joshua ben Levi,*
> *Rabbi Alexandri said: "One who sees the*
> *rainbow in the cloud should fall on one's face*
> *[and pray]."*
> —Babylonian Talmud, *Berakhot* 59a

*A*mong the 100 blessings that we are encouraged to recite each day is a blessing upon seeing a rainbow. The blessing goes something like this: "Thank you, God, for remembering the covenant" that you will not destroy the world again. Each time rains rage in the heavens, we are reminded of the dark clouds' inherent potential for destruction. And we want the rains to pass quickly. Yet, the rabbis warn us that the true enemy of Israel is the one who prays for a change in its weather. Endure the storm and wait for the rainbow to appear. Then you can offer up a blessing.

PERSONAL REFLECTIONS

_____

_____

_____

_____

_____

_____

The world is full of wonders and miracles, but
we take our little hands and we cover our eyes
and see nothing.

—The Baal Shem Tov

However understandable our fury may be, when we rage at everyone around us, we are unable to see the miracles of daily life that continue to sustain us—particularly at these times when we don't even realize it. In an ironic way, mourning opens our eyes to the world in a way that is different than any other period of time. If we engage in the formal thrice-daily prayer prescribed by traditional Judaism, then we are taken on a spiritual journey that provides us with a specific prism through which we can view the human encounter with the world. Or we can just be prompted to open ourselves up to the blessings of life by what we see around us. Either way, we'd better open up our eyes. The world has a lot for us to see.

PERSONAL REFLECTIONS

_____

_____

_____

_____

_____

*Let them make Me a sanctuary and I will dwell
in their midst.*

—Exodus 25:8

 Ⱥ ost people read this text from Exodus as God's instruction to build the portable tabernacle that would accompany the Israelites during their desert travels. Later,
our people used this as an impetus to build the ancient
Temple in Jerusalem. As humans, we always seem to
search for concrete ways to experience and express the
transcendent. But what if the text was translated a little
differently: "Let them make Me a sanctuary, *but* I will
dwell in their midst"? Would our response to God's instruction have been any different? In the midst of your
mourning, you need not run to the synagogue to confront
the Almighty to express your anger. For God is already in
your midst. God's sanctuary surrounds you; the sanctuary
is the very world in which we live.

PERSONAL REFLECTIONS

_____

_____

_____

_____

_____

Saturday/Shabbat _____ (today's date)

> *Oh, my suffering, my suffering!*
> *How I writhe!*
> *Oh, the walls of my heart!*
> *My heart moans within me.*
> —Jeremiah 4:19

*M*uch to the dismay of the priests, the prophet Jeremiah walked around ancient Jerusalem yoked at his neck. As the people ignored the degeneration of Jerusalem, Jeremiah wanted everyone to see how he suffered on her behalf. He taught us that when Jerusalem is troubled, every Jewish heart aches. By this time in your mourning, many people expect you to be well on your way to wholeness. But mourning is not a predictable process. The anger remains. Ancient sages and modern social psychologists alike have identified stages in mourning, and Jewish ritual reflects these stages. However, our spiritual and emotional lives are not so easy to anticipate. The yoke we bear may be visible to only a few, but we all share in its burden.

PERSONAL REFLECTIONS

_____

_____

_____

_____

A Meditation
Before Saying Kaddish

⟨∞⟩

*A*nd so it is that as the years come upon us, we gain a greater reverence for the flow of the generations. Our seeming wisdom only adds to the mystery of those who have come before, without whom we would not be, and through whom we seem to receive little pieces of some great image of being. We are increasingly impressed with the inherited knowledge of our ancestors. More reverent toward their heirlooms. Able now to listen to the legends with greater concentration: "Inquire of generations gone by, they will tell you; ask your parents, they will inform you" (Deuteronomy 32:7).

It is very easy. As simple as a father speaking to his son just after the boy has read from the Torah to become a Bar Mitzvah. He says, we love you and we are proud of you. You are our hope and our seed for the future.

And then he says to his grown-up little boy, I remember how your grandfather, my father, was there when you were born. And how he prayed he would live to see this day when you would read from the Torah. (But the old man is absent. Died many years ago. God, how he wanted to be here.) I am sorry, my son. Now it is only you and I. The chain goes on. May I live to be present when your children read from the Torah. And if it is not meant to be for me either, then please, will you say something like this for me? Everyone cries. Drops of water, you know, are a universal symbol for the resurrection of the dead.

—RABBI LAWRENCE KUSHNER,
THE RIVER OF LIGHT

Outrage

Sunday/Yom Rishon _____ (today's date)

Remember the Sabbath day by keeping it holy.
—Exodus 20:8

The Jewish people measure time in unique ways, depending on the occasion. We count lunar months and adjust them for the seasons. Mostly, we perceive each week through the designated Torah reading (and its complementary haftarah, specified for individual *Shabbatot* and holidays). We count the days of the ritual week relative to Shabbat, and thus Shabbat becomes a focal point for the entire week. As a result, we are instructed to spend each day preparing for Shabbat and anticipating welcoming her into our midst. Study helps us prepare for Shabbat, for it brings us closer to God. Whatever sacred literature you study today, use the text to begin your preparation for Shabbat. In it is a foretaste of the world to come.

PERSONAL REFLECTIONS

_____

_____

_____

_____

_____

_____

_____

Listen to Me, my people. Hear Me, my nation.
The law will go out from Me. My justice will
become a light to the nations.

—Isaiah 51:4

During the exile of our people from the land of Israel, Isaiah comforted them by saying that God has called us to be a "light unto the nations." Our acts of righteousness will lead a path for others in the world to follow. So perform a righteous act today and every day—and redirect your anger. The specific deed does not really matter. What is important is only that it helps ease another's burden. Whether you give *tzedakah*, help a stranger in need, or donate a few hours at a local soup kitchen, others will follow your example. Whatever you choose to do, do it to honor the memory of your loved one. Tell people why you are doing it. Thus, will their memory—and your action—be for a blessing.

PERSONAL REFLECTIONS

_____

_____

_____

_____

_____

_____

> *The wise person, his [or her] eyes*
> *are at the beginning,*
> *but the fool walks in darkness.*
>
> —Ecclesiastes 2:14

*A*ccording to the book of Ecclesiastes (which is called *Kohelet* in Hebrew), its author lived well into his old age. Because he lived a life of wealth and influence, tradition ascribes this work to the elderly King Solomon. I always imagined him as an elderly professor who kept a diary (more like a poet's chapbook) in which he jotted observations and insights—things that he had learned. In his old age, Ecclesiastes reviewed his life and all that he had learned. Sometimes, he agreed with what he had written. At other times, the perspective of time caused him to reject what he once held to be certain. So his instruction we take seriously: Rage is blinding. With it, we cannot see the truth—and not even the light.

PERSONAL REFLECTIONS

_____

_____

_____

_____

_____

_____

*Take us back, Adonai, to yourself, and let us
come back.
Renew our days as of old.*
—Lamentations 5:21

*B*ecause the Book of Lamentations (*Eichah* in Hebrew) is read during the observance of Tisha B'av, this text is closely associated with that holiday. Because of their incredible power to inspire the individual to action, these two lines of sacred text also made their way into the liturgy that is recited when we return the Torah to the ark after it has been read. Often the words are trampled by the choreography of the moment as people shuffle on their feet and finally sit down again. For me, saying these words from Lamentations is the most powerful part of the service. As I utter them, I close my eyes and am swept back to the desert when the Torah was revealed and our people journeyed in the desert. And I am renewed.

PERSONAL REFLECTIONS

_____

_____

_____

_____

_____

_____

*In blazing anger, You have cut down
all the mighty of Israel;
You have withdrawn Your right hand
in the presence of the foe;
You have ravaged Jacob like a flaming fire,
consuming on all sides.*

—Lamentations 2:3

*T*his is the way the author of Lamentations expressed himself (or herself) after experiencing the destruction of ancient Jerusalem. Defiant, the poet blamed God for the devastation brought to the golden city whom the Jewish people consider to be the spiritual center of the world. The memory lingers to this day. We thought that the city was indestructible. Then we learned that even Jerusalem could be burned, but only if God withdrew from her midst. Traditional Judaism suggests that through our actions, it was we who abandoned Jerusalem. We destroyed her through our own immoral acts. There was nothing left for our enemies to do, so God let them take her. As mourners, we remember our loved one along with Jerusalem, and we continue to do our work to take her back.

PERSONAL REFLECTIONS

_____

_____

_____

Friday/Yom Shishi   _____ (today's date)

The heaven and the earth were finished, and all
their array. . . . And God blessed the seventh day
and declared it holy, because on it God ceased
from all the work of creation which God had done.
—Genesis 2:1, 3

*T*he mystics who lived neared Meiron in Israel would gather in the open areas on a hillside to watch the sun set just as dusk settled each Friday evening—all in anticipation of the beckoning solitude of Shabbat. As the sun slowly descended on the horizon, these rabbis joined with everyday people from the community and recited the daily psalms in succession, one for each day of the week: Sunday, Monday, Tuesday. . . . Accompanied by *niggunim*, wordless chants and songs of *Kabbalat Shabbat* (or welcoming Shabbat), they recited the words of each psalm slowly and deliberately and reviewed each day of their week: its ups and downs, its pains and its pleasures, its successes and failures. Thus, they would prepare to invite Shabbat into their lives. As we remember our loved one, we invite Shabbat to infuse our spirits.

PERSONAL REFLECTIONS

_____

_____

_____

_____

For this is like the waters of Noah to me;
For as I have sworn that the waters of Noah
Should never again cover the earth,
So I have sworn that I would not be angry with
you, Nor rebuke you.

—Isaiah 54:9

*T*his is God's promise to the people as spoken through Isaiah. After the calamity of the Flood, recognizing the moral corruption of the people that precipitated it, God assured us that there would never again be such extensive destruction of humankind. Isaiah calls the Flood to mind as a warning to the people, simultaneously offering us hope and consolation. It reflects our relationship with the Divine, which is neither simple nor one-sided. We are responsible for our actions—and those actions might get in the way of our relationship, even if the relationship is not diminished in the process. It's not hard to initiate a relationship with God. But once it is established, it takes even more work to nurture. Particularly while we mourn, that's the part that requires the fullness of self.

PERSONAL REFLECTIONS

_____

_____

_____

_____

A Meditation
Before Saying Kaddish

⟨∞⟩

At each moment of our lives we encounter gates behind which beckons the unknown. We have little choice but to enter, and, as we do, the gate swings shut behind us. We can never go back. The known, the comfortable, the safe, all these are in the past; only the unknown, the dangerous, the mysterious and terrifying lay ahead. Moving on makes us human; doing so lightly and at peace makes us divine.

But, eventually, we come to the final gate, the final closing. The trail ends, leaving behind only memories of steps taken, leaps tried, grace achieved and shared. How do we mark this final gate? With tears and stories, with memories and love, with food and friends.

And with silence. Silence is the heart of death, and silence alone can do it justice. But silence does not mean passivity, and our tradition speaks of four virtues which form the core of silence.

The first is hearing: Hearing the inner voice of our pain and love; rejoicing that nothing, not even the grave, can rob us of that supreme human emotion.

The second is memory: Reclaiming the past by refusing to forget the joys once held. He or she who once lived among us now lives within us, and there our loved one cannot die.

The third is action: We must honor our dead by continuing to live ourselves. Their memory is quickened only in the fullness of our own lives, our own futures: our ongoing struggles to make sense out of an often senseless world.

The fourth is wisdom: Every life is a teaching, every person a guide to truth. We must allow the wisdom that was our loved one to become a part of ourselves, that (his/her) memory might lead us to an even greater wisdom of our own.

Hearing, memory, action, wisdom. . . . May each of these find a place in our silence, our grief, and our moving out again into the world where yet another gate beckons wide.

—Adapted from Rabbi Rami Shapiro

Wrath

Sunday/Yom Rishon _____ (today's date)

*You shall not oppress a stranger, for you know
the feelings of the stranger, having yourself been
strangers in the land of Egypt.*

—Exodus 23:9

The slave experience of Israel in Egypt contributed to the moral development of our ancestors, a spiritual legacy that we have inherited. During the forty-year journey of the Israelites through the desert, they reflected upon their enslavement and their deliverance by God. This experience shaped much of the behavior of the Jewish people as we traveled throughout history. We learned from having been strangers in many lands. Now that we are free—and have our own land—we are supposed to know how to treat one another, particularly strangers who come into our midst, if only to join our minyan to say Kaddish. In the context of saying Kaddish, there are no strangers—only friends.

PERSONAL REFLECTIONS

_____

_____

_____

_____

_____

Actively seek peace and pursue it.
—Psalm 34:15

Often when we read statements about peace, we assume that the writer is concerned with strife between nations. But the Psalmist understood the world in which he (or perhaps she) lived and wrote about conflicts between neighbors and friends, between family members and business associates. During the process of mourning, we have learned much about the friction in these relationships. When we confront potentially explosive situations, some of us have the ability to defuse them. The difficult process of mourning often diminishes this ability in us. When we least expect it, the Psalmist teaches that Jewish tradition asks more from us. We must actively seek peace. Regardless of the divergent paths we have traveled, we must look for ways to turn family members into friends once again.

PERSONAL REFLECTIONS

_____

_____

_____

_____

_____

_____

> *A psalm for You who causes others*
> *to be victorious.*
>
> —Psalm 13:1

*T*he Psalmist often gives us permission to say things that we feel otherwise uncomfortable or unwilling to say. Nevertheless, this text from Psalms seems to represent an unusual posture for even the Psalmist. Usually, we praise God—or express gratitude—for all that God has done for us or for others. Sometimes we recognize—even if we get angry—when our prayers go unanswered that not all of the prayers we utter are intended to result in our own well-being. We may be motivated to pray on behalf of others without any regard as to how these prayers will affect us. That's when we thank God for granting the prayers of others even at the expense of our own.

PERSONAL REFLECTIONS

_____

_____

_____

_____

_____

_____

_____

Do not rejoice when your enemy falls;
do not let gladden your heart when they stumble.
—Proverbs 24:17

*R*ejoicing about our foes' woes is a natural response against which we really have to fight. It's particularly true when we mourn, since people are more forgiving of us than usual for the things we say or do. Perhaps we unconsciously reason that we might feel better if others feel worse. Regardless of the state of our personal affairs, we have to remember the basic mandates that direct the interaction between individuals. Hillel said it best when he was challenged by a potential Jew-by-choice to teach the entire Torah while standing on one foot. "Do not do unto others what you would not want done to you," said the sage. "All the rest is commentary. Now go and learn it" (Babylonian Talmud, *Shabbat* 31a). Since study is part of the mourning process, it's time for all of us to do the same.

PERSONAL REFLECTIONS

_____

_____

_____

_____

_____

> *Ben Zoma said, "Who is wise? The one who*
> *learns from everyone as it is said (in Psalm*
> *119:99), 'Because everyone has been my teacher,*
> *I have gained understanding.'"*
>
> —*Pirke Avot* 4:1

*W*hatever the outcome of an event—good or bad—my colleague Rabbi Paul Steinberg constantly reminds me to "learn from the experience." He makes no distinction between the status of student or teacher. All are equal in the presence of the Torah of life. We all have something to offer from which others can learn. The perspective of growing older affirms that life itself is the greatest teacher. Perhaps this is a lesson we do not want to learn while still in the midst of our mourning and its message has been forced upon us. Residual anger can get in the way of any understanding. Ben Zoma said it clearly: Only when we realize that we can learn from everyone is real wisdom possible.

PERSONAL REFLECTIONS

_____

_____

_____

_____

_____

Friday/Yom Shishi _____ (today's date)

> *Remember this day, on which you went free from*
> *Egypt, the house of bondage, how Adonai freed*
> *you from it with a mighty hand.*

—Exodus 13:3

*S*acred memories are stored in the deep recesses of our minds, where they are merged with other experiences in our lives. Mourning causes our minds to flood with these memories, many of which we have not considered for many years. According to the Book of Exodus, Jewish tradition is not prepared to wait for a memory to surface on its own. Instead, we are frequently instructed to call to mind the experience of the Exodus and relive it. It even frames part of the core of the Friday evening Kiddush. As we mourn, we also recall the Exodus. Thus, we are taught to remember the Source of our deliverance, that God might deliver us once again.

PERSONAL REFLECTIONS

_____

_____

_____

_____

_____

_____

_____

Saturday/Shabbat _____ (today's date)

_Truly Adonai has comforted Zion, comforted all
her ruins; You have made her wilderness like
Eden, her desert like the Garden of Adonai._

—Isaiah 51:3

Following the late summer commemoration of Tisha
B'av, we read a weekly series of special haftarot that are
designed to help comfort the people for the historical loss
of the ancient Temples and Jerusalem. We relive that experience each year. So the first Sabbath following Tisha
B'av is named _Shabbat Nachamu_ because of the specific
haftarah portion of comfort. These verses from the
prophet Isaiah provide us with hope and inspiration at a
time in the calendar—as we recall the events of Jewish
history—when everything looks bleak. Instead of recalling the desolation we experienced, which might lead us to
despair or anger, the prophet Isaiah promises that we
might return to a time like Eden and enjoy the pleasures
of God's garden once again.

PERSONAL REFLECTIONS

_____

_____

_____

_____

_____

A Meditation
Before Saying Kaddish

⟨◦⟩

Death, what follows death, is a mystery defying imagination. Facing it, our language is silence. Yet while the body descends into the grave, trust remains, hope persists. . . .

Marvelous and beautiful is life in the body, but more marvelous and more beautiful is life in a word. The word is greater than the world; by the word of God all was created. The Book, Scripture, is an everlasting constellation of holy words. When a good man dies, his soul becomes a word and lives in God's book.

"And many of those who sleep in the dust of the earth shall awake, some to everlasting life and some to shame and everlasting contempt" (Daniel 12:2).

The decisive message of this passage is that death is not the final act, that there will be an awakening of those who sleep in the dust.

This is the hope that in dying I become a seed and that after I decay I am born again. Must the self remain the same rather than become the seed of a new self, a new being?. . .

The meaning of existence is in the sanctification of time, in lending eternity to the moments. Being human is a quest for the lasting.

Craving for God, longing for the immediate perception of the divine, for emancipation from selfish desires and inclinations—such freedom can only be achieved beyond death.

It is a distortion to characterize . . . life as moving toward death. Death is the end of the road, and while moving along the long road of days and nights, we are really moving toward living, acting, achieving. Death is the end of the road, but not its meaning, not a refutation of living. That every moment of life is a step toward death is a mechanical view. Every moment of life is a new arrival, a new beginning. Those who say that we die every day, that every moment deprives us of a portion of life, look at moments as time past. Looking at moments as time present, every moment is a new arrival, a new beginning. . . .

—Rabbi Abraham Joshua Heschel

Rancor

The sun rose upon him as he [Jacob] passed
Peniel, limping on his hip.

—Genesis 32:32

This line concludes the story that pits Jacob against the angel as they grapple with one another in the darkness of the night. Commentaries usually focus on the beginning of the story, but it is the conclusion of this narrative that gives the story its spiritual power. Imagine the scene: Joseph finds a place to rest for the night. He is weary from his journey. As he rests, he encounters this messenger from God, with whom he wrestles. After the struggle, the angel blesses Jacob. But the scene is not over. As the sun rises in the East, we see Jacob limping. He has been hurt. Even a Divine blessing comes with its costs.

PERSONAL REFLECTIONS

_____

_____

_____

_____

_____

_____

_____

The one who is obsessed with anger loses one's
image of God.
—Rebbe Nachman of Breslov, *Likkutei Etzot Hashem*

*E*ach of us has images or ideas of God based on the experiences of God in our lives. That's why our concept of God is multifaceted. This notion evolves over time. With each experience in our life, our image of God changes, sometimes only slightly. Thus, Nachman's warning is particularly instructive to us while we are still in the midst of mourning. It is not anger itself that Nachman warns against. He understands anger as a natural response to life's challenges. It is our potential obsession with anger that worries him. So he cautions us: Our anger risks our relationship with God. As we mourn, now is not the time to discuss theology when we need God most.

PERSONAL REFLECTIONS

_____

_____

_____

_____

_____

_____

_____

Rabbi Ilai'i said, "A person is known by three things: By one's cup, by one's pocket, and by one's anger. And some say: Also by one's laughter."
—Babylonian Talmud, *Eruvin* 65b

*W*hy would Rabbi Ilai'i choose these three things as the most important to observe in human behavior? It seems like a peculiar combination of attributes to warrant such attention from the rabbis. "One's cup" refers to the amount (of alcohol) one drinks or, better said, the amount one does not drink. In conventional idiom, we would say, "how we handle our liquor." "One's pocket" refers to the way one spends one's money. Is that person generous or miserly? Does he or she give to others in need? And "one's anger" refers to how a person reacts to difficult and trying situations. Rabbi Ilai'i believed that you could tell all you needed about a person by observing just these items. His colleagues remind us: In the midst of anger and pain, laughter releases the soul.

PERSONAL REFLECTIONS

_____

_____

_____

_____

_____

Wednesday/Yom Revii _____ (today's date)

> *Pinchas of Koretz taught: "Long ago, I*
> *conquered my anger and placed it in my pocket.*
> *I take it out when I need it."*

$\mathcal{S}$ome people believe that we can deny the reality of our anger entirely. Pinchas of Koretz recognizes the natural aspect of anger. But he wants to remind us that if we don't control our anger, it contains the potential to control us. But in order to control our anger, we have to acknowledge it, perhaps even embrace it, as part of the process of mourning. But, as we have learned, this stage of mourning is not restricted to a specified period of time. Our spiritual and emotional lives don't work that way. So, on occasion, following the advice of Pinchas of Koretz, we may feel free to release our anger and make use of it to grow. Out of anger can emerge healing.

PERSONAL REFLECTIONS

_____

_____

_____

_____

_____

_____

Thursday/Yom Chamishi _____ (today's date)

Rabbi Eliezer said, "Let your friend's honor be
as precious to you as your own."

—*Pirke Avot* 2:10

*T*his ethical principle is basic Jewish wisdom for living. Thus, it is in keeping with other advice such as "Love your neighbor as yourself" (Leviticus 19:18). That is why it was included in *Pirke Avot*, the book of the Mishnah devoted to aphorisms written by the rabbis and intended to guide our everyday life. However, this teaching is particularly apt to guide those in mourning (an inevitable state for all of us)—as we reflect on the one who has died and share stories with others about him or her. We now have an obligation to protect their honor even more than we did when they were alive. It is the responsibility of memory that we bear.

PERSONAL REFLECTIONS

_____

_____

_____

_____

_____

_____

_____

*I am Adonai, your God who brought you out of
Egypt to be your God. I am Adonai, your God.*
—Numbers 15:41

As a result of the retelling of the Sinai experience throughout the Book of Numbers, we are constantly reminded of the Exodus experience, a recurring theme throughout Jewish history, as well as Jewish sacred and secular literature: After years of slavery, God brought us out of Egypt. So we are reminded in this verse from the Book of Numbers. But the often overlooked phrase that follows is what captures the attention of the religious Jew. God brought us out of the "narrow places" of Egypt—which describes the mourning process as well—in order to be our God. God brought us out to develop a relationship with us. After 400 years of slavery, it was worth the wait. It still is!

PERSONAL REFLECTIONS

_____

_____

_____

_____

_____

_____

Saturday/Shabbat   _____ (today's date)

[It may seem like] I abandoned you
for a short moment,
But with a great compassion I will gather you.
—Isaiah 54:7

We are instructed to say Kaddish each day during the entire period of mourning. Regardless of the meaning of the individual words, the rhythmic cadence of Kaddish provides us with a way of affirming God particularly when we are angry and may feel that God abandoned us at the time of our greatest need. On Shabbat, as we sit in the synagogue with an empty seat next to us, we may feel this sense of abandonment most acutely: We are in God's house, yet feel most distant from God. It is quite a spiritual paradox. That's why Isaiah makes the promise to us: Not only will God gather us back, but God will do so with compassion (*rachamim*, which derives from the word *rechem*, "womb"), and we will feel welcome once again.

PERSONAL REFLECTIONS

_____

_____

_____

_____

_____

A Meditation
Before Saying Kaddish

⸺ ৩৩৩৩৩ ⸺

It is hard to feel serene when our world is not complete, when those who once brought wholeness to our life have gone. Yet in the emptiness their passing leaves behind, we are not alone. For we have the companionship of the living, and even our loved ones who have died live on in our hearts, for what they were is part of what we have become. We honour them best when we live, as they would wish, responsibly and happily, even in the shadow of our loss, and so draw closer to the Source of life, in whom life finds meaning, purpose, and hope.

—RABBI RICHARD LEVY

FOUR

Feeling Guilty and Making Deals

*Comfort you, oh comfort you My people, says your God
Bid Jerusalem take heart.*

—Isaiah 40:1–2
From the haftarah for *Shabbat Nachamu*,
the Sabbath of Consolation, which follows Tisha B'av

❧

*I*t is four months since you began the process of mourning. Your mind is still flooded with memories of those first moments. By this time, a measure of routine has returned to your life. Yet, some of those initial reactions remain with you. And you have come to realize that these feelings will never truly go away. Perhaps they will subside and lessen in their intensity and presence, but we know that they can return when you least expect it. But the profound pain you feel and the sense of loss never go away completely. They are just something you have to learn to live with as part of the price we pay for love and life.

This fourth stage of mourning is characterized by two perspectives. One seems to logically follow from the other. Regardless of how a person dies or their age at death—or even our relationship to them—we feel guilty. Your relationship with them did not work out exactly as you had planned. Our thoughts are eclipsed by "if onlys": "If only, I had. . . ." But that time is past and you can never recapture it. You may have attempted to make certain deals with God and yourself when your loved one was still struggling with dying. Perhaps part of the bargain you struck still weighs heavily upon you. The guilt we harbor spurs us to action.

But you are not alone in your struggle. The noted Hasidic rabbi, Simcha Bunam, once said, "We are instructed by God [in Exodus 30: 12] to give half a shekel as the ransom for our souls. Why only half? Because half of the guilt belongs to God for endowing us with the impulse to sin."

Remorse

Sunday/Yom Rishon _____ (today's date)

---

*Make yourselves holy, therefore,
and you will be holy.*

—Leviticus 11:44

*T*his sounds like a rather simple formula for something so significant at this stage of mourning. Through the Torah, God instructed the Jewish people to become "a realm of priests, a holy nation" (Deuteronomy 19:6). Our challenge is to determine how to do so. The spiritual logic that pervades Leviticus goes something like this: As long as we live a life wholly separate, then we can indeed reach the desired state of holiness. All it takes is a change in approach. And the details for this so-called attitude adjustment are contained throughout the Book of Leviticus. Our task is to probe the text in order to coax it to reveal its secret to us, to become the text, to be Torah.

PERSONAL REFLECTIONS

_____

_____

_____

_____

_____

_____

> *Alas, lonely sits the city once great with people.*
> *She that was great among the nations has*
> *become like a widow.*
>
> —Lamentations 1:1

*T*aken from the beginning of the Book of Lamentations (which is read as part of the observance of Tisha B'av), this text reflects the heart-wrenching pain of loss and separation. Jerusalem has been razed, and the people have been taken captive. All hope for the future seems to be lost. And here, from distant Babylonia, displaced exiles reflect on the grandeur and beauty that was once Jerusalem. They must do this through memory alone. The lingering guilt felt by the people from the early days of mourning (could I have done more?) is eclipsed by overwhelming feelings of sadness and melancholy, two emotions that reflect how we feel during this period of mourning. Yet, Jerusalem has now been reborn, her beauty has been restored. We have become her pilgrims, overcoming challenge so that we can climb the mountains and sit at her gates once again.

PERSONAL REFLECTIONS

_____

_____

_____

_____

> *Our masters taught, "A person should always*
> *regard oneself as though half-guilty and*
> *half-meritorious."*
> —Babylonian Talmud, *Kiddushin* 40b

After four months of mourning, why do we still feel guilty? Why are we now motivated to make deals with God and ourselves after so much time has passed? Seeking the answers to these questions helps us understand the challenge of the mourning process. Through this searching, we understand the wisdom of the sages, perhaps more so now than ever before. We can't expect that the process of mourning logically unfolds and develops. In fact, there is no logic to it at all. We all bear responsibility for the quality of life and death, some more than others. None of us are free of it, yet we are all meritorious, for we remember our responsibility to the deceased to carry on their memory and the good work that they have done.

PERSONAL REFLECTIONS

_____

_____

_____

_____

_____

No one ascribes guilt to oneself.
—Babylonian Talmud, *Shabbat* 119a

$\mathcal{S}$hould the text be read as "No one *should* ascribe guilt to oneself"? Or perhaps, "No one ascribes *enough* guilt to oneself." This talmudic statement seems like an obvious statement, what some people like to call a "no-brainer." It appears to be self-evident in the context of a legal system. It also looks like it reflects the attitudes of the general public. If that's the case, then why did the sages include this statement in the Talmud, especially if it conflicts with the feelings of mourners? That's their point. By reminding us that "no one ascribes guilt to oneself," the rabbis take us beyond this current stage of mourning and back into the ranks of daily living. Because of the clarity of their wisdom, our inner self can be saved.

PERSONAL REFLECTIONS

_____

_____

_____

_____

_____

_____

_____

Thursday/Yom Chamishi _____ (today's date)

> *You are not a God who desires to declare guilt.*
> —Psalm 5:5

Each encounter with God teaches us a little about the Holy One. It is part of our ongoing attempt to gain knowledge even in the face of the infinite nature of the Divine. Likewise, each challenge we confront teaches us about our own ability to rise above obstacles that stand in the way of our growth. These challenges test our inner strength. Abraham was said to have ten trials, each of which proved his inner strength while simultaneously nurturing his relationship with God. We already learned many things during mourning. Now it is time to learn one more thing about God: The Holy One does not desire that we declare our guilt. Rather, God wants us to simply live lives of blessing.

PERSONAL REFLECTIONS

_____

_____

_____

_____

_____

_____

Friday/Yom Shishi _____ (today's date)

> *Then I will remember my covenant with Jacob . . .*
> *and I will remember the land.*
>
> —Leviticus 26:42

*J*ewish tradition has always been focused on the land, recognizing since the time of Eden that we have to live in harmony with it. The land supports us only if, in return, we are willing to nurture it. The rabbis even say that we have an obligation to plant a tree even if we will probably not be alive to enjoy its fruit. And that whenever a child is born, a tree should be planted and its branches will be used years later to form the *chuppah*, the wedding canopy, at the wedding of the full-grown child. As we enhance our relationship with nature, we remember that the one we mourn is now part of the earth for which we care.

PERSONAL REFLECTIONS

_____

_____

_____

_____

_____

_____

Scarce are they planted, scarce are they sown,
scarce has their stock taken root in the earth.
When You blow upon them, they wither
and the whirlwind takes them away like stubble.
—Isaiah 40:24

Often we see Jewish history reflected in the journeys of our own families. However you choose to read Jewish history, this has been the lot of our people. Yet, it has survived and prospered. You, too, will survive and prosper. This is the prophet's message to the people that is carried through history to us during our mourning—even if it is still hard to hear after four months of mourning. Isaiah wants us to understand that suffering takes place only when we are unwilling to find meaning in our pain. Then the suffering has no purpose. And death is for naught. That is one reason why Judaism helps guide us through this period. It is difficult to think about in these terms, but even in death, we can find hope.

PERSONAL REFLECTIONS

_____

_____

_____

_____

_____

A Meditation
Before Saying Kaddish

〜

To every thing there is its season, a time for every purpose under heaven:

a time to be born, and a time to die;
a time to plant, and a time to uproot;
a time to kill, and a time to heal;
a time to pull down, and a time to build up;
a time to weep, and a time to laugh;
a time to mourn, and a time to dance;
a time to scatter stones, and a time to gather them up;
a time to embrace, and a time to let go;
a time to keep, and a time to throw away;
a time to tear, and a time to mend;
a time for silence, and a time for speech;
a time for love, and a time for hate;
a time for war, and a time for peace.

—Ecclesiastes 3:1–18

Contrition

> *We will do and we will hearken.*
> —Exodus 24:7

This text has puzzled Jewish scholars for centuries. The enigmatic response of the Israelites upon receiving the Torah is, indeed, a peculiar reaction to revelation. Notice the order of the verbs. The Israelites were prepared to do what was asked of them by God before they even fully understood the content of the Torah. This reflects the traditional Jewish notion that action will lead to understanding. We do mitzvot because they are asked of us—even if we don't quite (yet) understand them. Mourning is not the time to engage in an intellectual discussion about the meaning of theodicy. But the lesson of revelation remains the same. Do what the tradition asks of you during this time—and you will come to understand.

PERSONAL REFLECTIONS

_____

_____

_____

_____

_____

_____

_____

> *But wisdom, where shall it be found?*
> *And where is the place of understanding?*
> —Job 28:12

*M*ourning forces upon us various opportunities to gain insight and wisdom about life and human suffering, although we would have preferred that this learning come through other means. While there may have been people who spent time with us during the early days of mourning, particularly during the period of shiva, they have returned to their normal routine, anticipating that we would soon do the same. We find ourselves more alone now as the months since the death of our loved one have unfolded. This gives us more time to think and reflect. We may feel somewhat guilty, as did Job, because others are in greater distress than us. Nevertheless, we understand Job's questions in ways we never did before. Mourning is part of life's journey, a journey we must take to truly attempt to understand life.

PERSONAL REFLECTIONS

_____

_____

_____

_____

_____

Tuesday/Yom Shelishi _____ (today's date)

> *My heart pierces [my soul] within it.*
> —Psalm 109:22

The pain returns when we least expect it. We have no choice but to acknowledge it. As much as we would like to believe otherwise, mourning does not follow a specific pattern or path. It does not carefully copy the journey that others have taken. There are similar moments, to be sure, and other people will offer you insights from their own experience. But mourning—even in community and with the support of family and friends—is something we must eventually face alone. Rituals will soften the pain. Jewish life will help place that pain into a context. And the Psalmist, as she does so often in our tradition, provides us with words when we do not know how to speak and gives voice to our inner pain.

PERSONAL REFLECTIONS

_____

_____

_____

_____

_____

_____

> *One is forbidden to pray that the wicked be*
> *removed from the world.*
>
> —*Zohar* I, 105a

*W*hy has it taken us four months to feel guilty? Why are we only now making "deals"? We may have felt guilty during the early days of mourning, particularly in the very painful, intense first days after the death. But in the flood of those emotions, we were not able to tell one emotion from the other. Now, with the perspective of time, we can begin to reflect on the myriad of emotions (anger, isolation, longing, relief) we experienced, including guilt. Now we understand the wisdom of this text from the *Zohar*. How many times did we say things or do things regarding the deceased that we now regret? Wicked or good, life is beyond our control. Our life—and the eternal life of the one we mourn—are both in the hands of God. What better place can there be?

PERSONAL REFLECTIONS

_____

_____

_____

_____

_____

_____

Thursday/Yom Chamishi _____ (today's date)

I have sinned. I have transgressed.
I have acted perversely.
—High Holiday *Mahzor*

According to Rabbi Joseph B. Soloveitchik, a leading contemporary theologian who taught at Yeshiva University, a Jew comes to the synagogue on the Day of Atonement and uses the ancient language of the High Priest's confessions. He or she begins, "I have sinned, . . ." and then is wracked by suffering. He or she lists his or her sinful acts that are due to a sense of spiritual emptiness and disasters. On that Day of Atonement, the Almighty accepts such suffering as a qualified sin-offering. His sins are considered atoned for. So he can now "'re-purchase' himself and make a new start in life." It may not seem that way now, but mourning readies us to begin again.

PERSONAL REFLECTIONS

_____

_____

_____

_____

_____

_____

_____

Friday/Yom Shishi _____ (today's date)

And they stood under the mount.
—Exodus 19:17

As a result of the revelation of Torah at Mount Sinai, the Jewish people is called the chosen people. Because of its sensitive nature, this topic is generally avoided in liberal religious circles. Rabbi Mordecai Kaplan, the founder of the Reconstructionist movement in Judaism, rejected the idea of chosenness completely and reconstructed the liturgy to reflect this understanding. He believed that the Jews did the choosing, not God. This discomfort was not new to the twentieth century. In one midrash, the rabbis say that God held Mount Sinai over the heads of the Israelites and offered them the choice of Torah or the mountain: life or death. They chose life so that we might all live. We can do no less.

PERSONAL REFLECTIONS

_____

_____

_____

_____

_____

_____

Behold, days are coming and I will send
a famine in the land,
But the famine will not be for bread,
And the thirst will not be for water,
But to hear the word of God.

—Amos 8:11

*A*mos is generally known as the prophet of doom in Jewish tradition. This perception comes primarily as a result of his dismal prophecies on the future fate of Israel. In this particular selection, he offers the Israelites an interesting twist on what we have come to expect from him. He provides us with a striking lesson for living, one that comes at an important juncture in the mourning process. We need not worry about famine or thirst because they will be of a surprising nature. Nor need we make any deals about our lives. Our bodies will hunger for God. We will thirst for words of Torah, the sweet elixir of life. In our longing for both, we will be sated.

PERSONAL REFLECTIONS

_____

_____

_____

_____

_____

A Meditation
Before Saying Kaddish

⟨══⟩

*W*hen a person is born, everyone rejoices; but when a person dies, the entire community weeps. It doesn't seem like it should be that way. When a person dies, there is cause for rejoicing, especially if he leaves the world in peace with a good name. It is as if there are two ships, one leaving the harbor and one entering it. As one sailed out of the harbor, everyone on shore rejoices. Yet, no one displayed any joy over the ship that enters the harbor. In observing this scene several times, one teacher said, "There is no cause for rejoicing over the ship that leaves the harbor. No one knows her plight, what seas and storms she may encounter. Yet, the ship which enters the harbor has successfully weathered the storm. Thus, we can rejoice that she has returned safely. Likewise, when one dies, we should all rejoice and offer thanks that he gracefully departed the world with a good name."

—*KOHELET RABBAH* VII, 1:4

Bargaining

Sunday/Yom Rishon _____ (today's date)

You saw no shape when Adonai, Your God
spoke to you at Horeb out of the fire.
—Deuteronomy 4:15

This is a restatement of one of the most powerful visions of God by any human. As you may recall, Moses had encountered God in the midst of a bush that burned yet was not consumed by the fire. Much of Moses' life had prepared him for that moment. He had learned to see God's face and to hear God's voice. Recognizing that he was on holy ground, he removed his shoes. In the midst of mourning, if we learn how to listen—something that the long process of mourning prepares us for—then we, too, can hear God's voice. But here's the real challenge of the moment: God was not *in* the fire. God *was* the fire.

PERSONAL REFLECTIONS

_____

_____

_____

_____

_____

_____

When you see a beautiful tree or person, one should say, "Blessed is the One who has created such beautiful creatures in the world."
—Jerusalem Talmud, *Berakhot* 9:2

*S*aying a blessing is one way that we affirm God's presence in our lives. Judaism has evolved a specific formula to use with one goal in mind: to bring the person into a relationship with God. This phrasing is a poetic way prescribed by Jewish tradition to say, "Thank you, God, for bringing this blessing into my life." It is not enough to just recite the blessing when we happen upon a situation that requires it. Rather, the rabbis encourage us to search out opportunities to offer these blessings. They understand the dilemma of mourning. The blessing above is particularly important to say at a time when we don't feel as if there is much beauty in the world or much reason to even offer a blessing. That's reason enough to speak such words of prayer.

PERSONAL REFLECTIONS

_____

_____

_____

_____

_____

Through charity, I behold Your face.
—Psalm 17:15

*C*harity, which is a loose translation of the Hebrew word *tzedakah*, is more about righteous giving than about making a donation to someone in need. It is one of the acts that is encouraged during mourning to honor the memory of the deceased. Moses Maimonides, the great medieval Jewish philosopher, said that there are eight levels of charity. The greatest form of *tzedakah* is anonymously providing funds to a person so that he or she might become independent and no longer need charitable contributions. From an ethical point of view, *tzedakah* is about redistributing wealth in the world in a just way. What is most amazing about the whole process is that in the face of the one who gives and the one who receives is the reflection of the Divine.

PERSONAL REFLECTIONS

_____

_____

_____

_____

_____

_____

> *Rabbi Hama bar Hanina said, "The righteous*
> *are more powerful after their death than*
> *during their life."*
> —Babylonian Talmud, *Hullin* 7b

*T*orah takes many forms, which are not restricted to the sacred scrolls housed in the synagogue ark. Individual lives can become sacred texts as well. This particular form of Torah lives far beyond the grave. Thus, we understand the power of bar Hanina's words, even though we may feel guilty about acknowledging that they are true. Prior to mourning, we may not have even taken bar Hanina's words seriously. Now we take them to heart. The Torah that our loved one taught by how he or she lived continues to influence our lives and the lives of others in significant ways and often when we least expect it. These lessons forge new links in the chain of tradition that secures the future. It ensures a life after death for the one we loved and lost.

PERSONAL REFLECTIONS

_____

_____

_____

_____

_____

Thursday/Yom Chamishi _____ (today's date)

*Hezekiah said, "A person's prayer is not heard
until you make your heart [soft] like flesh."*
—Babylonian Talmud, *Sotah* 5a

Our prayers take many forms. Whether or not they follow the fixed routine of liturgy and worship, our prayers are now reflecting the variety of emotions we feel during mourning. Sometimes, they are angry and embittered. At other times, they are demanding and petulant. Oftentimes, our prayers are silent, echoing only in the recesses of the heart. Hezekiah's lesson is profound in its simplicity. The specificity of prayer is unimportant. When we are out of words to say and no printed prayer reflects what we truly need to say, then we simply speak what is in our heart. God makes sense out of what we have to say even when we are unable to do so ourselves.

PERSONAL REFLECTIONS

_____

_____

_____

_____

_____

_____

Friday/Yom Shishi _____ (today's date)

God remembered Abraham and removed Lot.
—Genesis 19:29

*E*arly in the Torah, Abraham argued with God over the fate of Sodom and Gomorrah even though they both understood how corrupt these two cities were. Could two large cities contain no one worthy to be saved? It is a powerful scene, one of Abraham's best moments in the entire Torah. Although he was unable to save the cities from the destruction they themselves wrought, his righteous indignation provided us with a model to follow. It was not Abraham's power of persuasion that caused God to act and save Lot and his family. It was Abraham's merit that saved Lot—even more than Lot's own actions. This is what the Torah comes to teach us. Through our own merit, we may have the ability to save another. That is what we believe even as we confront the death of the one we love. Because God remembers the merit of what we have done.

PERSONAL REFLECTIONS

_____

_____

_____

_____

_____

I am the first and the last,
Before Me there is no other.

—Isaiah 44:6

*S*ome people claim that Judaism has neither creed nor catechism, that Judaism has no unyielding dogma that can be taught in a series of ready-made statements. While this perspective is generally an accurate reflection of historical Judaism, this statement of Isaiah provides us with a basic insight into Jewish theology that is somewhat contradictory to this rather narrow view. Remembering that God speaks through the voice of the prophet, Isaiah's words offer us an opportunity to affirm our own belief, even at a difficult time in the mourning process. God is a unique presence in the way we reckon the history of the world. Even better said, God is the history of the world.

PERSONAL REFLECTIONS

_____

_____

_____

_____

_____

_____

_____

A Meditation
Before Saying Kaddish

⸻ ❧ ⸻

Sorrow is the obverse side of love. To ask for immunity from sorrow is to ask for more than a special dispensation granted no other. It is to ask that we do not experience love, gain no friends or devotedly serve any cause. To enter into any relationship of deep meaning is to run the risk of sorrow. When we become parents or link our life to another's or find a friend to whom we are closer than brother or sister, we inevitably expose ourselves to the pangs of separation or the grief of injury or illness or to a death. But let us for a moment consider the alternative. One meets people whom life has wounded deeply. Fate has dealt them a harsh blow: A dear one died. A friend betrayed a trust. A hope failed to be fulfilled or a kindness was repaid with ingratitude. Life is not going to find an exposed flank in their case. They will not open their hearts in trust; they will not permit acquaintance to ripen into friendship; they are prepared to forgo love, family, children. They are resolved that no human being will become so dear to them that their death will bring grief. They protect themselves against sorrow. But they also shut out the possibilities of joy and companionship, the richest and most vital satisfactions of life.

But such surrender does not necessarily indicate deepest feeling. There are people whose self-pity is greater than their grief and who in mourning replace the object of their sorrow with their own hurt.

We shall be helped in maintaining our balance during life's trials if we remember that sadness is the universal heritage of mankind. The contingency of pain is the only condition on which love, friendship, and happiness are ever offered to us. This recognition is the hallmark of maturity.

—Adapted from Rabbi Morris Adler

Negotiation

Sunday/Yom Rishon _____ (today's date)

Your right hand dashes the enemy into pieces.
And the waters piled up with the
blast of your nostrils.

—Exodus 15:6b; 8a

God can be a powerful advocate as much as a gentle friend. Throughout the Torah, we read of God's prowess in war, destroying the enemy on our behalf. In this verse from Exodus, we read of how God destroyed the Egyptians who enslaved us. As a result of God's military might, our ancestors eventually left Egypt, crossed the Red Sea, and journeyed in the desert before reaching the Promised Land. That is what we have to anticipate. Their journey took great faith, although their faith wavered while they were in the desert. The process of mourning is similar to the desert journey of our ancestors. But who is the enemy we are waiting for God to destroy? Perhaps it is the remorse we feel.

PERSONAL REFLECTIONS

_____

_____

_____

_____

_____

_____

Monday/Yom Sheni _____ (today's date)

Pain and suffering should lead to liberation.
—Babylonian Talmud, *Berakhot* 5a

*C*onsider the travels of the Jewish people throughout their history. Often, the journey was bleak, marked by pain and suffering. At other times, it felt like Eden once again. Communities grew and flourished. Somehow, we survived and prospered. And now, we enjoy freedom in our own land and in others. Even in the darkest periods of our history, Divine light eventually illuminated the path for our ancestors—as it will for us. Like most of us, the rabbis of the Talmud look for meaning in suffering. During mourning, we do the same. And at the end of the process, we can anticipate liberation. We may feel guilty about our impatience—but we are in a hurry to be redeemed.

PERSONAL REFLECTIONS

_____

_____

_____

_____

_____

_____

_____

It is not in our power to explain either the
prosperity of the wicked or the afflictions
of the righteous.

—*Pirke Avot* 4:19

*M*ourning is not the time to intellectualize. People offer us comfort but are afraid to ask questions that challenge our belief in God. However, after four months, nagging questions are beginning to surface that we avoided asking earlier in our bereavement. These are the kinds of questions that Jewish teachers have been puzzling over for generations. They are the questions that the contemporary liturgist Rabbi Lawrence Hoffman likes to call "the real questions in life." Just asking them reveals wisdom in itself. The sages who wrote in *Pirke Avot* understood our questions. They lived in the same world that we do. Like us, they do not have the answers. Also like us, they are committed to searching for them.

PERSONAL REFLECTIONS

_____

_____

_____

_____

_____

_____

*A person is forbidden to eat before he [or she]
has fed his [or her] animals.*
—Babylonian Talmud, *Berakhot* 40a

$\mathcal{W}$e may not give it much thought, but the lesson from *Berakhot* represents a primary Jewish principle. We share this world with trees, plants, animals, humans. This idea from the Talmud reflects the precept of *tzaar baalei chayim*, "prevention of cruelty to living creatures." It is one of several fundamental constructs that form the foundation for kosher dietary laws. Whether we are talking about work animals or those we have slaughtered for food or domesticated animals that have become members of our families, we have a responsibility to all of God's creatures, particularly those that are under our care. It is particularly important to remember this talmudic teaching during the entire period of mourning, when we tend to focus more on ourselves. We must remember to take care of ourselves, as well. The well-being of others depends on our own.

PERSONAL REFLECTIONS

_____

_____

_____

_____

---

*If God did not conceal from each person the day
of his death, no one would build a house and no
one would plant a vineyard because each person
would say, "Tomorrow I will die, why should
I work for others?"*

—*Yalkut Shimoni* on Ecclesiastes, section 968

*W*ould we live our lives differently if we knew the day
of our death? This is not an easy question. The *Yalkut
Shimoni's* (a comprehensive anthology of midrash) discussion of it evolves directly from the experience of the
author of Ecclesiastes, whom the tradition suggests is
King Solomon. Ecclesiastes wondered why he should
work so hard if he was not able to reap the benefits of his
labors. Instead, those who come after us, who did not
exert themselves, will enjoy the gain. But that's precisely
the point. We work for those to come after us. The Talmud reminds us that if we are busy planting a tree and
the Messiah arrives, we should finish planting before running to greet him—so we might all enjoy its fruit.

PERSONAL REFLECTIONS

_____

_____

_____

_____

𝒻riday/Yom Shishi _____ (today's date)

Remember Abraham, Isaac and Israel [Sarah,
Rebecca, Leah and Rachel], Your servants to
whom You did swear by your own self.
—Exodus 32:13

𝒮ometimes, we have to remind God of God's responsibilities. Some might think that this smacks of limiting God and making God seem less powerful. On the contrary, this affirms God's powerful presence in the world. God's reminders to us usually come in the form of mitzvot. We are both partners—with responsibilities—in our covenantal relationship. Sometimes we don't feel that we can stand on our own merit when addressing God so we have to rely on what our ancestors did (what tradition calls *zekhut avot*, the merit of our ancestors)—and remind God of God's own promise to them on our behalf. This is not part of the deal we now make with God. Instead, it is the deal God made with us.

PERSONAL REFLECTIONS

Saturday/Shabbat _____ (today's date)

*I will gather the remnant of my flock from all the lands
of their dispersion and I will bring them back to their
land and they will multiply and be fruitful.*

—Jeremiah 23:3

*T*he prophet Jeremiah brings us these words from the
midst of exile. But it is a promise that is fixed in neither
time nor place. We live in lands throughout the world
and transcend the borders of sovereign nations. This is
what historian Jacob Rader Marcus likes to call "omni-
territoriality." Jeremiah's words brought us hope wherever we lived. They provided direction for us when we
thought that such inspiration was impossible. They followed the Jewish people throughout our wanderings.
Sometimes we feel guilty about where we have chosen to
live, away from families and relocating because of pres-
sures of profession or occupation. During mourning,
many of these feelings are heightened. But God's words
travel through the centuries and speak directly to us now
so that we can return home.

PERSONAL REFLECTIONS

_____

_____

_____

_____

A Meditation
Before Saying Kaddish

⟋⟋⟋⟋

Birth is a beginning
And death a destination.
And life is a journey:
From childhood to maturity
And youth to age;
From innocence to awareness
And ignorance to knowing;
From foolishness to discretion
        And then perhaps to wisdom;
From weakness to strength
Or strength to weakness—
        And often back again;
From health to sickness
        And back, we pray, to health again;
From offense to forgiveness,
From loneliness to love,
From joy to gratitude,
From pain to compassion,
And grief to understanding—
        From fear to faith;
From defeat to defeat to defeat—

until, looking backward or ahead,
We see that victory lies
Not at some high place along the way,
But in having made the journey, stage by stage,
  A sacred pilgrimage.
Birth is a beginning
And death a destination
But life is a journey,
A sacred pilgrimage—
  To life everlasting.

      —RABBI ALVIN FINE

FIVE

Out of the Depths
I Call to You

I found trouble and sorrow,
but I still called upon the name of Adonai.
—Psalm 116:3–4

ᕳᎷᎷᏅ

*M*ourning tests our faith in ways unlike anything else that we experience in our lives. It may come as a surprise when we realize that faith in God often grows and matures when we face our greatest moments of disbelief. Often our religious beliefs are affirmed in unusual ways. The traditional rituals of mourning bring us into frequent contact with God, slowly building and nurturing the covenantal relationship that was established by our ancestors at Sinai. In the process of mourning, we are reminded that our mortality is a shadow of God's divinity. And so we call out to God for solace and support, for hope and inspiration. At times, we also call on the Divine out of desperation. We know not where else to turn. Nevertheless, we come to realize during this fifth month since the death of our loved one that the process of mourning, while frequently painful, helps to restore our faith. As

Rabbi Hama bar Hanina said, "If a person sees that he [or she] prays and is not answered, he [or she] should pray again, for Scripture [Psalm 27:14] says, 'Wait for Adonai and be strong; let your heart be courageous. Indeed, wait for Adonai'" (Babylonian Talmud, *Berakhot* 32b).

Real prayer, whether fixed and routine, or spontaneous and random, must come from the inner reaches of our souls. This is the way our tradition sees it: "A person's prayer is not answered until one places one's entire life in God's hands, as it is said [in Lamentations 3:41], 'Let us lift up our hearts with our hands to God in the heavens'" (Babylonian Talmud, *Taanit* 8a). The prayers that we encounter in prayer books let us use the words of others until we are able to form our own. The psalms that shape much of our liturgy also give us permission to say things to God we didn't think were possible.

WEEK ONE
Longing

O God, why have You done evil to this people?
—Exodus 5:22

While this text may be unique to a particular moment in the Torah, following an increase in the Israelites' burden after Moses' first appeal to Pharaoh, it reflects a familiar refrain from the Israelites while they wandered in the desert. Regardless of what God does for the people one day, they complain to Moses about their lot the next moment. In this instance, Moses asks God: Why did God redeem the Israelites from Egyptian slavery only to let them struggle in the desert? Now, in the midst of our mourning, we ask the same thing of God. Moses and the people didn't understand why they had to suffer. Perhaps this is the real reason that they—including Moses—were prevented from entering Canaan. But we must understand our journey. It was not the redemption from Egypt that freed us. It is the desert struggle that makes us free.

PERSONAL REFLECTIONS

_____

_____

_____

_____

_____

> *Remember: Nothing begets wholeness in life*
> *better than a heartfelt sigh.*
> —Rebbe Nachman of Breslov, *The Empty Chair*

*T*his is the kind of profound "kitchen table" wisdom that makes Rebbe Nachman so popular today. He taught people to focus the spiritual energy that resides in their body to bring healing. He believed that some of these elements were part of a *tikkun klali*, a complete remedy for the body and soul. (Jewish tradition does not make a separation between the body and the soul. They both form our essential core.) And there were a variety of ways that Rebbe Nachman recommended for us to achieve wholeness. In one place, he selected numerous psalms to read: 16, 32, 41, 42, 59, 77, 90, 105, 137, 150. His message was simple: Express yourself to God. Find the path to the Divine so that you may continue to live.

PERSONAL REFLECTIONS

_____

_____

_____

_____

_____

_____

Rabbi Joshua ben Levi said, "One who gladly accepts the sufferings of this world brings redemption to the world."
—Babylonian Talmud, *Taanit* 8a

While knowing that we don't suffer in vain provides us with a measure of solace, it does not lessen our pain or our sense of separation and loss. Nevertheless, it does help to know that, in some way, perhaps in a way that we may never fully understand, we are participating in God's plans for the world. So we pray that God may give us insight and understanding so that we may better understand. But Rabbi Joshua ben Levi, who taught much about our role in the redemption of the world, asks us to cheerfully endure our suffering. Is it perhaps because he knows that suffering paves the way into the next world?

PERSONAL REFLECTIONS

_____

_____

_____

_____

_____

_____

For my part, I will not speak with restraint. I will
give voice to the anguish of my spirit. I will
complain in the bitterness of my soul.

—Job 7:11

*F*or most people, it is difficult to compare their circumstances, however painful, to Job's experiences as described in the Bible. Perhaps our situation is similar to the talmudic tale that describes a person who complained about his poverty. This individual was so poor that he could not even afford to buy shoes. And so, he walked barefoot. Then he met a person who had no feet—and he complained no longer. But Job did no wrong. He was the victim of a power struggle between God and Satan. It was not Satan who lost; it was Job. Like him, as mourners, we have the right to say anything to God—and to offer God the painful prayer that is in our heart.

PERSONAL REFLECTIONS

_____

_____

_____

_____

_____

_____

> *All the streams run into the sea.*
> *Yet the sea is not full.*
>
> —Ecclesiastes 1:7

*J*ewish tradition ascribes the Book of Ecclesiastes to King Solomon. I believe it is the work of a lesser known figure who "lived the life of a king." The comment above reflects part of his general view of life, the kind of view that mourning forces us to undertake. The midrash *Ecclesiastes Rabbah* (1:7) explains this text so that we may all come to understand its wisdom: "All of human wisdom is nowhere other than in the heart. 'Yet the sea is not full'— the heart is never filled to capacity. You might suppose that when a person lets one's wisdom go forth from the heart [like when one teaches another], it will never flow back to the individual. 'Yet all streams flow back again.'"

PERSONAL REFLECTIONS

_____

_____

_____

_____

_____

_____

_____

Friday/Yom Shishi _____ (today's date)

> *It is not in heaven.*
>
> —Deuteronomy 30:12

*U*sually this text refers to the Torah, but in the midst of our mourning, it evokes other issues for us. The answers to our questions, the ones that have plagued us these last five months—and will continue to do so throughout this year, if not throughout our entire lives—may not be in the heaven (so as to be beyond our reach). Instead, as the verse continues, they are here on earth so that we might find them on our own. But how do we know where to look? And is that where we will find God? According to philosopher/theologian Martin Buber, we find divinity in our relationships with others. These relationships mirror our relationship with the Divine—and thus we find the holy in our midst.

PERSONAL REFLECTIONS

_____

_____

_____

_____

_____

_____

Saturday/Shabbat _____ (today's date)

I am weary from my sighing, and I can find no rest.
—Jeremiah 45:3

We certainly understand Jeremiah's lament. After five months of mourning, we too are tired of complaining, but we seem to have no choice. We are exhausted even at the start of a new day—which is supposed to feel like the beginning of rebirth. It feels beyond our control. But Shabbat is the one time where we can, indeed, find that rest. Death takes place within the confines of time. The next world, of which Shabbat offers a foretaste, is beyond time. Thus, if only for twenty-five hours (which is how we count Shabbat time), we can suspend our mourning—and simply live. For that, says our tradition, we are provided with an extra soul that joins our own and fortifies it.

PERSONAL REFLECTIONS

_____

_____

_____

_____

_____

_____

_____

A Meditation
Before Saying Kaddish

⟨⟨⟨⟩⟩⟩

*J*udaism . . . teaches us to understand death as part of the Divine pattern of the universe. Actually, we could not have our sensitivity without fragility. Mortality is the tax that we pay for the privilege of love, thought, creative work—the toll on the bridge of being from which clods of earth and snow-peaked mountain summits are exempt. . . . Because we are human, we are prisoners of the years, yet that very prison is the room of discipline in which we, driven by the urgency of time, create.

We can face death without dread when we learn that the Angel of Death plays a very vital role in life's economy. Actually, there could be no growth, no progress, if generations did not come and go. There also would be very little meaning to existence if the years were not marked off in the calendar of time by childhood, adolescence, youth, and age. There is a time to run gaily with all the intense excitement of a boy with flushed cheeks racing on a summer's day toward the winding river of sport and adventure; there is also the time when that boy, transformed by the alchemy of the years into an old man, no longer seeks to run but is quite content to sit and browse even unto the twilight.

—RABBI JOSHUA LOTH LIEBMAN

Hunger

No human is God.
—Numbers 23:19

While this appears to be an obvious statement, the rabbis remind us that each word is in the Torah for a reason. Even the spaces between the words have something to teach us. And we, says the tradition, are supposed to honor the one who teaches us a verse, a word, even a letter of Torah. This verse from Numbers contains a teaching that we relearn each difficult day during mourning. We are endowed with many godlike qualities. We should try to emulate the ways of the Divine. Nevertheless, we can never *be* God, even as we strive to become one with the Divine. Alas: The Holy One of Blessing is immortal, but we, so our mourning reminds us, are not.

PERSONAL REFLECTIONS

_____

_____

_____

_____

_____

_____

I am racked with grief;
sustain me in accordance with Your word.
—Psalm 119:28

*I*n their frank honesty and openness, the words of the Psalmist provide us with solace. Often we repeat them over and over as a *kavannah* (a Jewish mantra) for mourning. Yet, no matter how poetic are the words that are offered, even the Psalmist recognizes that they provide us with only a limited measure of comfort. The pain remains; only God can truly comfort us. We know that God has a reputation to maintain. The Torah provides us with a record of Divine interactions with the world. And the Psalmist tells us about her personal encounters with God. So we ask of God only one thing: Sustain us as You sustained our ancestors, whom You promised that You would do for us.

PERSONAL REFLECTIONS

_____

_____

_____

_____

_____

_____

---

*Rabbi Eleazar ben Azariah said, "If there is no
wisdom, there is no fear [of God]; if there is no
fear [of God], there is no wisdom. If there is no
knowledge, there is no understanding; if there is
no understanding, there is no knowledge."*

—Pirke Avot 3:17

*T*he rabbis of *Pirke Avot* were known for their profound insights into daily living. They sought to provide
us with guidance for routine life and avoid the esoterica
of philosophical discourse. So whether we translate the
Hebrew in Rabbi ben Azariah's quote above as "fear" or
"reverence," as is often the case, we can readily determine its relationship to wisdom and knowledge, particularly in the midst of mourning. It is precisely at this time
of our greatest need that we understand the wisdom im-
plicit in establishing a relationship with God. Through intimate knowledge of God, real wisdom may be revealed
to us. And there we find strength.

PERSONAL REFLECTIONS

_____

_____

_____

_____

_____

As the garden, so the gardener.
—Genesis *Rabbah* 80:1

*T*his is a simple statement that resonates throughout Jewish tradition. We encounter it in the early days of creation as the world evolves under God's careful guidance. We meet it as Adam and Eve frolic in the garden—and are eventually expelled from it. We sense it in the various agricultural laws and celebrations that follow the journey of the Israelites throughout their wanderings. We sense it even in the various customs of mourning that mark our individual communities. We ourselves experience it as we move through each year's cycle of seasons and reconnect with the land, eventually emerging as a people on a land that overflows with milk and honey. How we treat God's creation is reflective of who and what we are. Most importantly, it reflects what we can yet become.

PERSONAL REFLECTIONS

_____

_____

_____

_____

_____

_____

> *Rabbi Sheshet used to go over his studies every*
> *thirty days. Then he would stand up, lean on the*
> *bar of his doorway, and say: Rejoice, O my soul,*
> *rejoice, O my soul! For your sake, I have read*
> *Scripture, for your sake I have studied Mishnah.*
> —Babylonian Talmud, *Pesachim* 68b

*S*tudying sacred text is part of the regular routine of the religious Jew and one of the many ways through which an individual can come to know God. When two people study, say the rabbis in *Pirke Avot*, the Divine Presence rests among them. The blessing for study (which carries you throughout the day) is even included in the daily blessings said upon waking each morning. And, as we have learned as part of the ritual of our bereavement, study is prescribed at various times in order to focus our thoughts and reaffirm our relationship with the Divine. But we study for other reasons, as well, since Torah, as Rabbi Sheshet understands, is also a healing balm. *Zil g'mor*: Go and study—and may you be renewed.

PERSONAL REFLECTIONS

_____

_____

_____

_____

For it is the Lord God who marches with you to do battle for you against your enemy to bring you victory.

—Deuteronomy 20:4

The enemy. Usually the word conjures up images of foreign powers threatening to do us evil. In our day, it recalls the horrors of the Holocaust, the ongoing struggle of the State of Israel, and the occasional flash of anti-Semitism. But the rabbis offer us a different perspective. They claim that the enemy does not strike from the outside. The enemy is within. It is the *yetzer harah*, the inclination to do evil that resides in each of us and is brought into balance only by the *yetzer tov*, the good inclination. With God's help, we must be vigilant even while we are mourning, for the *yetzer harah* knows no boundaries. It is not the spirit of power that brings us victory. Rather, it is the power of the spirit.

PERSONAL REFLECTIONS

_____

_____

_____

_____

_____

_____

Saturday/Shabbat _____ (today's date)

> *There is hope for the future. . . . My children will*
> *return to our borders.*
> —Jeremiah 31:17

*I*n exile, Jeremiah brought the people undying hope. When Jerusalem was a distant memory, he envisioned the day when we would all come home and celebrate her grandeur once again. Shabbat is a day filled with such optimistic vision. It anticipates a world yet to be created. Shabbat bolsters our confidence in God even when our faith in the world and in ourselves is waning. Some say that in the light of Shabbat you are able to see all the way from the time of creation to the coming of the Messiah. Others say that the Sabbath candles actually illumine the path of the messianic. This ultimate promise for the world offers us comfort during mourning as we patiently wait for its blessing.

PERSONAL REFLECTIONS

_____

_____

_____

_____

_____

_____

A Meditation
Before Saying Kaddish

⟨⟩

Whatever science or reason may ever say about the nature and persistence of matter, the more profound wisdom of the heart will guarantee the immortal life of our dear ones. But how they live—the quality of the influence they radiate—depends not alone on the kind of life they lived. It depends as much on us. We, the living, can determine the kind of immortality our beloved shall have. We can be more selective than they were when they lived among us. They had to compromise with the needs of the flesh and of the hour. Their good was mingled with the bad; the fine with the gross. We can sift the dross. We can recreate them as the fury and heat of their earthly life would not permit. We can grant renewed life to their nobler insight and their finest visions. We can act as their personal representatives to the living. Where they lifted the burden of worry from a fellow man, we can give encouragement and help; where they brought cheer and care and loyalty, we can be instead. That is how we can bind them into the bundle of eternal life, and build for them a memorial more enduring than stone, sweeter than the rose.

—*Adapted from* Rabbi Jacob J. Weinstein

Yearning

> *He shall say to them, "Hear O Israel, You are*
> *about to do battle with your enemy. Do not let*
> *your courage falter. Do not be in fear, or in*
> *panic, or in dread of them."*
>
> —Deuteronomy 20:3

This sounds like the guidance of a general sending out troops into battle. It seems out of place in the Torah even as the Israelites continue their battle to settle the Promised Land. Look at his choice of words above: "Hear O Israel," the same phrase that is spoken twice a day during routine prayer and once before going to sleep at night. Hear O Israel, *listen* to God. If you do, your courage will not falter nor will you be in fear of any enemy. For God is with you in all your battles whether the enemy threatens from *outside* or from the deepest recesses of your soul. Stand guard and you shall emerge victorious. God is on your side, so listen for the Divine voice speaking to you in your grief.

PERSONAL REFLECTIONS

_____

_____

_____

_____

_____

Monday/Yom Sheni _____ (today's date)

> *Rabbi Menachem Mendl of Vitebsk said,*
> *"Rejoice that you have an opportunity to sing*
> *unto God."*
>
> —*Midrash Ribesh Tov* 49

*L*ike much of the spiritual wisdom of Hasidic teachers, this insight of Menachem Mendl is profound in its utter simplicity. He understands the pain of loss. We all do. In the midst of mourning, there may be little cause to rejoice. However, that is precisely the reason that we must force ourselves to do so. As survivors, we have the responsibility to sing songs of praise to God for those who are no longer able to do so. There is no great honor than to carry their song forward on our lips. So says the tradition: "May the words of my mouth and the meditation of my heart be acceptable to You, O God, my Rock and my Redeemer."

PERSONAL REFLECTIONS

_____

_____

_____

_____

_____

_____

Tuesday/Yom Shelishi _____ (today's date)

*Thus did Rabbi Judah: When he would behold a
wedding or a funeral procession passing by, he
would call the attention of the disciples to it and
say: Doing takes precedence over learning.*

—*Semachot* 11

Given Jewish sensitivity to mourning and bereavement, it may be surprising to learn that if a funeral procession encounters a wedding party in the middle of the street, the wedding is always given precedence. As a matter of fact, it must *take* the right of way. The overall rule is basic and extends to most other things: Life takes precedence over death. Feeling this dominant focus on life was inadequately expressed, Rabbi Judah was dissatisfied with the extent of that teaching that funerals must stop for weddings. He wanted to teach his students the lesson that we must all learn: Talking about ritual—even discussing its theological consequences—is not enough. Jewish life is not in the knowing; it is in the doing.

PERSONAL REFLECTIONS

_____

_____

_____

_____

_____

God is called Makom *["space"] because God is*
the space of the universe.
—*Bereishit Rabbah* 68:9

*M*oses Maimonides, one of the greatest Jewish philosophers and theologians argued that we should avoid listing God's attributes, since no listing can be complete. He called this the "theory of negative attributes," and he went so far as to say that listing attributes actually took away from God's significance rather than added to it. The text from the midrash cited above lists no attributes of God. Instead, the rabbis offer one descriptive statement of God that is, by far, one of the most moving and comforting. In our mourning, God provides us with a space in which we may feel sheltered. That place *is* God.

PERSONAL REFLECTIONS

_____

_____

_____

_____

_____

_____

_____

Thursday/Yom Chamishi _____ (today's date)

*One should proclaim God's unity with one's lips
by reciting the* Shema. *One should feel it in one's
heart; one should think of it in one's mind.*

—*Zohar* 1, 242a

The *Shema* is close to being the central Jewish statement because it expresses the basic religious foundation
of Judaism. It includes the personal name of God (pro-
nounced in its original form only once a year by the High
Priest on Yom Kippur) and the mention of God in the
form of awesome power. In this prayer alone, these two
polar experiences of God are brought together. For the
Zohar, the primary book of Jewish mysticism, the understanding is substantiated in two ways. The understanding
of God must be felt in the heart and in the mind.
Through applying both—especially during mourning—
we have experienced both the personal and the awesome
nature of the Divine and we come to know God.

PERSONAL REFLECTIONS

_____

_____

_____

_____

_____

_____

You shall love God with all your heart, with all
your soul, with all your might.
—Deuteronomy 6:5

This is a familiar text that we usually read too quickly and, thus, spend little time reflecting on its instruction to us. It is the basic "how to" for living the spiritual life. The text introduces the paragraph that immediately follows the two lines we think of as the *Shema*. Technically, several paragraphs make up the full *Shema* in the prayer book. In each paragraph, the underlying theme expressed in this text from Deuteronomy is the same: Love of God is a process. Love is all-consuming and has the potential to lift us to the very vault of heaven. I know it; I've been there. As we have learned through mourning, to engage the process, one must employ the entire being: our heart, our body, and our soul.

PERSONAL REFLECTIONS

_____

_____

_____

_____

_____

_____

> *I raised up prophets from among your children,*
> *and Nazirites from among your young.*
> *Is this not so, people of Israel?*
> *—says Adonai.*
>
> —Amos 2:11

*A*ccording to the Bible, a Nazirite was an individual who dedicated himself to God. Usually, the vow of the Nazirite was for a limited time and applied to a particular situation. It was a way of expressing to God thanks for the blessings of individuals or families. The vow always included abstention from wine and other alcoholic beverages, from unclean food, and from cutting one's hair. It was possible for parents to dedicate their children for their entire lives to being a Nazirite. In gratitude for his birth, for instance, Samson's parents dedicated him as a lifetime Nazirite. But what does it take to be a modern Nazirite? How does one dedicate oneself to God? And what have we learned in the process of mourning that might motivate us to do so?

PERSONAL REFLECTIONS

_____

_____

_____

_____

A Meditation Before Saying Kaddish

⚭

Our sorrow can bring understanding as well as pain, breadth as well as the contraction that comes with pain. Out of love and sorrow can come a compassion that endures. The needs of others hitherto unnoticed, the anxieties of neighbors never before realized, now come into the ken of our experience, for our sorrow has opened our life to the needs of others. A bereavement that brings us into the lives of our fellow-men writes a fitting epilogue to a love that had taught us kindliness and forbearance and had given us so much joy.

Sorrow can enlarge the domain of our life, so that we may now understand the triviality of the things many pursue. We have in our hands a noble and refined measure for judging the events and objects we daily see. What is important is not luxury but love; not wealth but wisdom; not gold but goodness.

And our sorrow may so clear our vision that we may, more brightly, see the God of Whom it was said, "The Lord nigh unto them, that are of a broken heart." Beyond the hurry and turmoil of life rises the Eternal. There is God in a world in which love like ours could bloom. There is God in a world in which human beings could experience tenderness. There is God in a world in which two lives can be bound together by a tie stronger than death.

Out of that vision will come a sense of obligation. A duty, solemn, sacred and significant, rests upon us. To spread the love we have known to others. To share the joy that has been ours. To ease the pains that man's . . . malice inflicts. We have a task to perform. There is work to be done and in work there is consolation.

Out of love may come sorrow. But out of sorrow can come light for others who dwell in darkness. And out of the light we bring to others will come light for ourselves—the light of solace, of strength, of transfiguring and consecrating purpose.

—*Adapted from* Rabbi Morris Adler

Desire

Sunday/Yom Rishon _____ (today's date)

> *When they say to me, "What is the Name?,"*
> *what shall I tell them?*
>
> —Exodus 3:13

*T*his question frequently challenged Moses. Feeling inadequate in his own right, he depended entirely on God and often on others. So he constantly pressed God for information and assistance. When Moses needed help, God sent Aaron along to help him speak to Pharaoh. We understand Moses more now than we ever did, especially since we have faced challenges throughout this period of mourning. Maybe his weakness is what gave him his strength as a leader. Even after experiencing an intimate relationship with God, Moses was without words. Words are often inadequate to express everything that is in our hearts. Moses was unable to express what he experienced. So he groped for words, for a name, for anything that might identify God for others. And then he continued on his mission to free his people. We may stop along the way, but then we must continue as well.

PERSONAL REFLECTIONS

_____

_____

_____

_____

Monday/Yom Sheni _____ (today's date)

> *The name of the righteous is to be*
> *invoked as a blessing.*
>
> —Proverbs 10:7

*A*s names are read as we prepare to say Kaddish each day, this phrase is often repeated: *Zekher tzadik livrakha,* "The memory of the righteous is a blessing." It is a liturgical formula that offers us comfort in the midst of our pain. But this text from Proverbs is more instructive. It suggests that we actually invoke the name of the deceased as a blessing for us. In other words, we deserve to be blessed because of his or her good works in the world. And we indeed are blessed because of what he or she really did. The deeds were sometimes simple, but their impact on us was profound. It is part of the odd nature of spiritual logic, but we are, indeed, blessed by his or her passing.

PERSONAL REFLECTIONS

_____

_____

_____

_____

_____

_____

> *No monuments need to be put up for the*
> *righteous. Their words are their monuments.*
> —Jerusalem Talmud, *Shekalim* 2:5

As we approach the midpoint in our first year of mourning, it is time to think about unveiling the stone that marks the final resting place of our loved one. We will probably spend a great deal of time thinking about the intricate nature of that stone, for we recognize that the stone will communicate the righteous living of our loved one to all who visit. We may want to build the largest stone, one that soars above the rest. And while we may want to spend a great deal of money as an expression of love, it is important to heed the advice of the rabbis of the Jerusalem Talmud: The words and deeds of the righteous are monument enough.

PERSONAL REFLECTIONS

_____

_____

_____

_____

_____

_____

God understands all the shapings of thoughts.
—1 Chronicles 28:9

*E*ven when we are unable to place into words the prayers of our hearts, God somehow understands. A disciple of Rabbi Levi Yitzchak of Berditchev, a great Hasidic teacher, complained that a newcomer to the community was standing in the back of the congregation mumbling the letters of the *alef-bet* over and over again. When Levi Yitzchak pressed the stranger, it seemed the man had wandered far from Judaism and only returned in order to say Kaddish for a parent. But all he could remember of his studies from youth was the Hebrew alphabet. And so Levi Yitzchak told the disciple: These are the most honest and heartfelt prayers heard in this synagogue in many years. May we all learn from this holy man.

PERSONAL REFLECTIONS

_____

_____

_____

_____

_____

_____

_____

> *Rabbi Papa said that there is no grief in the*
> *presence of the One who is everywhere, for*
> *Scripture [1 Chronicles 16:27] says, "Strength*
> *and joy are in God's place."*
> —Babylonian Talmud, *Hagigah* 5a

*T*hese five months have been filled with mourning rituals and marked by the disparate emotions that punctuate the phases of our bereavement. Without warning—and sometimes in the course of only a few moments—we experience emotional swings from the depths of despair to the heights of exhilaration. From the pangs of our grief has begun to emerge a renewed perspective about our evolving relationship with God. In helping us to reach the Divine, Jewish ritual has also provided us with stability and comfort during the difficult transition from life to death and back to life again. A talmudic rabbi, Rabbi Papa teaches: When you acknowledge God's presence in your life, there is no grief. There is only strength and joy.

PERSONAL REFLECTIONS

_____

_____

_____

_____

_____

Behold there is a place by Me.
—Exodus 33:21

This is an open invitation by God originally extended to the Israelites during their journey through the desert. During their sojourn there, they experienced frustrations and disappointments. They were often ready to turn back to Egypt. In the desert, we learned that no matter how far you travel and no matter how far away from God you wander, there is always a place reserved for you next to the Holy One. This is one of the things that we realize during mourning, even those among us who have strayed far from the basic rites and rituals of Judaism: God wants us nearby. God yearns for our prayers. So let your prayers be heard. God is waiting to listen.

PERSONAL REFLECTIONS

_____

_____

_____

_____

_____

_____

Saturday/Shabbat _____ (today's date)

The righteous shall live by his [her] faith.

—Habakkuk 2:4

$\mathcal{E}$ach time we recite Kaddish, we consider the meaning of righteousness. The prophet's words ring true to our experience. Through our faith in God, however difficult it is to maintain during the trying times of mourning, we affirm God as the source of all righteousness. One way we hold on to the memory of the one we lost is by recalling the acts of goodness they performed. We need not build memorials for them, since these have already been built out of the actions of their own lives. How we now choose to live in the reflection of their memory, by what they taught us through their lives, defines the parameters of faith for us. By their righteousness, we all live.

PERSONAL REFLECTIONS

_____

_____

_____

_____

_____

_____

A Meditation Before Saying Kaddish

There is perhaps no struggle that is harder for us than our struggle to face mortality. The grief we feel with bereavement challenges us to say good-bye, to find our way back to the rhythms of life among friends and community, and to discover new paths toward the Eternal that knows no death. That is why, as a community, we ask those whom loss has touched to lead us in sanctifying the Eternal. May their struggle help us find renewal for our lives, and for our actions, in holiness.

—JEFF GOLDWASSER

SIX

Introspection

The soul of a human is the lamp of God,
searching all its innermost parts.
—Proverbs 20:27

Jewish tradition offers us frequent opportunities to look inside ourselves and probe the deepest recesses of our soul. The Jewish calendar is dotted with holidays and observances throughout the year that provide us with occasions for growth and renewal. And on *Rosh Chodesh*, the new moon, at the beginning of each month, we review the weeks that have ended to help us prepare for the month ahead. It is necessary but hard work; it is, in fact, the only way to grow. Then at the end of each year, our tradition instructs us to devote the entire month of Elul (late August/early September) to fully evaluating our self and attempting to repair our relationships with others. Only then can we stand before God and be judged for what we have done throughout the year.

Similarly, the death of one we love forces us to take a good, hard look at ourselves and the life we have been leading. As we took the covers off the mirrors in our homes at the end of the week of shiva, we looked squarely into our own eyes. This honest self-analysis allows us to consider our relationships with others as well.

Often death encourages the renewal of our relationships with those from whom we have been estranged, especially relatives and friends.

As we begin this month, we ask the difficult question prompted by the process of mourning: What are we now prepared to change about our lives in the days ahead as we slowly return to the regular routine of daily living?

Soul-Searching

*All the congregation lifted up their voice and
cried, and the people wept that night.*

—Numbers 14:1

*A*s the Israelites journeyed through the desert, they encountered many obstacles along the way. Often these encounters frightened or dispirited them, and they wept bitterly through the night. Under Moses' guidance, they were often able to look honestly at their journey and at themselves. This process provided them with the insight and determination to continue their journey. Like the desert sojourn of our ancestors, mourning is also a journey. An important part of that journey includes the willingness to search the self even in the specter of our pain. As the Torah teaches us: It was the collective voice of the people that provided individual comfort, but we also have to be willing to listen to one another.

PERSONAL REFLECTIONS

_____

_____

_____

_____

_____

_____

Monday/Yom Sheni _____ (today's date)

This I recall to my mind, therefore I have hope.
—Lamentations 3:21

When the Israelites were exiled from Jerusalem, the memory of her capture seared unforgettable images into their souls. However, these visions of Jerusalem also brought them comfort; it helped to keep her memory alive even when they were so distant from her. When they were gone from her soil, they were able to more fully understand their relationship with her. When we take the time to look inside ourselves and search our memories, we discover many things about the deceased, even if not all of them are pleasant and we may not want to call them to mind. Yet by doing so, our deceased—and his or her relationship with us—is given life through our memories. These recollections give us hope for the future and strengthen us.

PERSONAL REFLECTIONS

_____

_____

_____

_____

_____

_____

> *Rabbi Abbahu bar Ze'era said, "Great is*
> *repentance, for it preceded the creation of the*
> *world, as it is said, 'Before the mountains were*
> *brought forth . . . You turned men [and women]*
> *to contrition' (Psalm 90:2–3)."*
> —*Genesis Rabbah* 1:4

*S*elf-scrutiny paves the path for repentance. It is how we repair ourselves, our relationships with others, and ultimately the world. Repentance may not come easily, but it is an indispensable part of healing. It's one of the reasons that God built it into the very fabric of the world—even before creation. It may seem like an odd topic for bereavement. However, just as death diminishes us, mourning renews us and provides us with time to reflect on ourselves in light of the one we have lost. As we consider the actions of the deceased through this process of introspection, we have the potential to change—and, by our actions, we can transform the memory of the one we lost into a blessing.

PERSONAL REFLECTIONS

_____

_____

_____

_____

Do not pry into things too hard for you
Or examine what is concealed from you
Meditate on the commandments you have been given
What Adonai keeps secret is no concern of yours.
—Ben Sira 3:21

The writings of Ben Sira, which are included in the second century B.C.E. Jewish wisdom literature, are among the most perceptive in the entire Bible. He consistently offered uncanny insight into the human condition. His advice is profound in its piercing simplicity. As you spend this month searching the self, you will undoubtedly uncover many things that you don't—and may never—understand. Ben Sira suggests that we just let go of these difficult issues. In time, we may come to understand some of them. Others—which he attributes to God—may always elude us. In the meantime, it is better for us to meditate on the commandments, since they will bring us to God and to ourselves. That is what will bring understanding.

PERSONAL REFLECTIONS

_____

_____

_____

_____

> *Hillel said, "If I am not for myself, who will be*
> *for me? But if I am only for myself, what am I?*
> *If not now, when?"*
>
> —*Pirke Avot* 1:14

*T*his, the most well-known of Hillel's teachings, provides us with the perfect prism through which to see this phase of mourning. As we look deeply into ourselves, we may be overwhelmed by self-doubt and plagued by such questions as, Did I do the right thing? Is it too soon to do something for myself? Others will certainly offer us advice during our mourning, trying to help and comfort in their own way, but the challenge of readjusting to life during mourning and after is ultimately ours to face. Take Hillel's advice to heart: Take care of yourself but not at the expense of others. Now is the best time to take a step forward, and the best way to do that is by just placing one foot in front of the other and moving ahead.

PERSONAL REFLECTIONS

_____

_____

_____

_____

_____

In the image of God they created the human.
—Genesis 9:6

*I*n the early days of mourning, particularly as it is required by Jewish law, others cared for us. They provided us with meals. They arranged for others to gather so that we could say Kaddish. We were not even permitted to take care of many of our daily needs, like preparing meals for ourselves. Slowly, as the mourning process continued beyond shiva, the well-meaning support ended as friends and family returned to the lives they had interrupted to help us and to mourn with us. But truthfully, we have spent little time over the last few months taking care of ourselves because we were so focused on our loss. The Torah wants to remind us, however, that the responsibility to take care of ourselves has a Divine origin and that this godlike responsibility to care for the self is holy.

PERSONAL REFLECTIONS

_____

_____

_____

_____

_____

_____

*Rejoice with Jerusalem . . . join in her jubilation
all you who have mourned for her.*

—Isaiah 66:10

*T*he prophet spoke of Jerusalem from the distance of exile in Babylonia. But his message might just as well have been written today. That is part of the power of Isaiah's message and the mesmerizing hold of Jerusalem over all who have encountered her. To walk the streets of Jerusalem is to instantly fall in love with her. Perhaps only those who have done so can truly understand why Jewish tradition links personal rituals of mourning to the collective mourning of the Jewish people for the destruction of Jerusalem two thousand years ago. As we mourn for our own deceased, we mourn for Jerusalem. And as we celebrate Jerusalem's rebirth, we are comforted for our personal loss.

PERSONAL REFLECTIONS

⎯⎯⎯⎯⎯⎯⎯⎯⎯⎯⎯⎯⎯⎯⎯⎯⎯⎯⎯⎯⎯⎯⎯

⎯⎯⎯⎯⎯⎯⎯⎯⎯⎯⎯⎯⎯⎯⎯⎯⎯⎯⎯⎯⎯⎯⎯

⎯⎯⎯⎯⎯⎯⎯⎯⎯⎯⎯⎯⎯⎯⎯⎯⎯⎯⎯⎯⎯⎯⎯

⎯⎯⎯⎯⎯⎯⎯⎯⎯⎯⎯⎯⎯⎯⎯⎯⎯⎯⎯⎯⎯⎯⎯

⎯⎯⎯⎯⎯⎯⎯⎯⎯⎯⎯⎯⎯⎯⎯⎯⎯⎯⎯⎯⎯⎯⎯

⎯⎯⎯⎯⎯⎯⎯⎯⎯⎯⎯⎯⎯⎯⎯⎯⎯⎯⎯⎯⎯⎯⎯

A Meditation
Before Saying Kaddish

⟡

In every person there is a private shrine of memory
and love, and in that sanctuary our loved ones
abide. We sense their presence, caress their spirits,
and enfold them in our hearts. They talk to us; they
tell tales. Thus, the pain of separation is soothed by
memory, the hurt sustained is healed by love; and
we ourselves become purified and ennobled through
our sorrow.

—RABBI JACOB K. SHANKMAN

Self-Examination

And Moses sat to judge the people.
—Exodus 18:13

*T*hroughout their desert journey, the Israelites constantly sought counsel from Moses. He offered personal guidance to all who came to see him until his father-in-law, Jethro, suggested that he should delegate the responsibility to others. So Moses established a court system and a counsel of elders. After that, only the most difficult cases were brought to Moses. Each decision that Moses rendered came only after he examined himself in relationship to the decision. When we mourn, we are tempted to judge others who did not adequately express their sympathy to us or come to comfort us at all. But Moses knew that before he could judge others, he first had to judge himself. And that that was the most difficult task of all.

PERSONAL REFLECTIONS

_____

_____

_____

_____

_____

_____

_____

A righteous person who submits to the wicked is like a fountain that gets muddied or a spring that becomes polluted.

—Proverbs 25:26

*M*ourning presents us with many personal challenges that we are forced to face. We confront personal obstacles that we previously might not have known. We may not even have had the strength to overcome them were it not for the inner reserve we discovered during mourning. We become stronger as a result. In the process of self-examination that takes place during mourning, we learn many things about ourselves. Some of these occur spontaneously; others we will learn about either as they evolve or we reflect back on them. However, not all of them are things that we wanted or were prepared to learn. We may be tempted to bring our discoveries to others for their evaluation and scrutiny, but by doing so, we run the risk that the writer of Proverbs warns us against. Just be careful.

PERSONAL REFLECTIONS

_____

_____

_____

_____

_____

The one who does good to one's own person is a person of piety.

—Proverbs 11:17

As we mourn, we focus on the deceased, but often, we neglect ourselves. And that raises the concern of others. We don't eat; we don't sleep. That's one reason why the writer of Proverbs shares this wisdom with us. But there is more. Our entire selves are gifts from God: body and soul, both brought together for our sojourn on earth. Thus, we have the obligation to care for the body, for it is the vessel in which our soul thrives. But the soul must also be nurtured at a time when our world feels diminished. By attending to our souls, we can raise the level of holiness in the world. That draws us closer to God through attention to the Divine that is in us.

PERSONAL REFLECTIONS

_____

_____

_____

_____

_____

_____

_____

Three things restore a person's spirits: sounds,
sights, and scents.
—Babylonian Talmud, *Berakhot* 57b

This seems like a peculiar statement from the rabbis of the Talmud—particularly at this time during the mourning process. At this moment, we are only beginning to come to terms with our new station in life. What we experience during mourning are reflections of life in the world that God created. Death, therefore, becomes the shadow, the reverse of all that is living in the universe and for all that we offer thanks to God: The sound of a newborn's laugh. The sight of young lovers. And the scent of spring in the air. They do not take away the pain of mourning. In fact, nothing can really do so. However, they do restore us and give us the courage to move on. And so, too, does the mourning process, in accord with ancient Jewish wisdom, take us from death to life once again.

PERSONAL REFLECTIONS

_____

_____

_____

_____

_____

Let others praise you but not your own mouth.
—Proverbs 27:2

*M*ore wisdom from the writer of Proverbs, whom tradition names as King Solomon. As a result of its popularity, there are many who have commented on this verse. Rav Papa, a Babylonian teacher who lived from about 300 to 375 C.E. and was probably an editor of the Talmud, said, "But if there are no others, then it must be with our own mouth." Sometimes we learn something about ourselves that we need to bring to the attention of others. Sometimes things that we had accepted as fact for many years are subject to new scrutiny during mourning. We may also learn during this time that things were really not the way they seemed and that we were not the way people thought that we were. So we have learned to sing our own praises.

PERSONAL REFLECTIONS

_____

_____

_____

_____

_____

_____

You shall not go over this Jordan.
—Deuteronomy 3:27

With these words, God answers the question that Moses pondered as he led the people through the desert: Would he join the Israelites in the Promised Land? Like many of us, he was unable to fully realize his dreams. This dialogue between Moses and God takes place in the annual Torah reading each year right after Tisha B'av, when the Jewish people mourn the destruction of Jerusalem. To offer comfort, God allows Moses to climb a mountain and look over the Jordan so that he might see where the people will live. In an insightful commentary on the scene, Rabbi Sheldon Zimmerman suggests that this, indeed, provides him comfort, since it gave Moses the vision to see what all his work had wrought, even if he could not directly experience it.

PERSONAL REFLECTIONS

_____

_____

_____

_____

_____

_____

Saturday/Shabbat _____ (today's date)

> *Let the heart open that it might bear the fruit of*
> *redemption with righteousness in blossom at its side.*
> —Based on Isaiah 45

*I*n a unique approach to time that simultaneously hearkens back to Eden and looks ahead to *mashiach-zeit* (messianic time), Shabbat offers us a foretaste of the world-to-come. And the only investment we make is time: Friday evening and Saturday. As we embrace Shabbat, we can find the seeds for personal redemption that may bear fruit for the rest of our lives. We carry these seeds into the workaday world and plant them wherever we go in whatever we do. The prophet Isaiah offers us guidance for Shabbat and for our lives, especially during this introspective period in our mourning. Particularly at this time, when your heart seems so vulnerable, open your heart so that you can find redemption.

PERSONAL REFLECTIONS

_____

_____

_____

_____

_____

_____

A Meditation
Before Saying Kaddish

꘎꘎꘎

ℱor the leader, a Psalm of David.
Adonai, You have examined me and know me.
When I sit down or stand up, You know me.
You discern my thoughts from afar.
You observe my walking and reclining
and are familiar with all my ways.
There is not a word on my tongue
but that You, Adonai, know it well.
You have protected my front and my flank,
and have given me guidance.
Such knowledge is too awesome,
it is too difficult for me to reach.

Where can I escape Your inspiration?
Where can I flee from Your presence?
If I go up to heaven, You are there.
And if I escape to Sheol, you are also there.
If I fly on the wings of dawn,
And inhabit the farthermost point of the sea,
Even there, You would guide me;

Your strong hand would support me.
If I say, "The darkness will envelop me,
And the light of night surrounds me,"
Even the deepest darkness is not too dark for You.
Instead, the night is as bright as the day,
Darkness is illuminated by light.

—Psalm 139:1–12

Self-Analysis

Sunday/Yom Rishon _____ (today's date)

---

*Cursed be the one who does not allow the words
of this Torah to stand.*

—Deuteronomy 27:26

*M*any people prefer not to discuss the curses that are in the Torah. Certainly, it would be easier to ignore the dark side of the Torah and concentrate only on words of blessing and fulfillment. However, the Torah's darkness reflects the reality of life. Some understand the passage above to refer specifically to the words of the Torah itself. However, the Hebrew text also refers to the works of Torah, those deeds that emanate from the text and, therefore, extend it. We may not want to express it as bluntly as does Deuteronomy, but a curse is nothing more than the absence of blessing that is readily available to anyone. The writer of Proverbs said it all: Torah "is a tree of life to those who uphold it" (Proverbs 3:18).

PERSONAL REFLECTIONS

_____

_____

_____

_____

_____

_____

*A rebuke to a person of understanding goes
deeper than a hundred lashes on a fool.*
—Proverbs 17:10

*W*hile Jewish law, custom, and tradition guide us, we still make many personal choices during mourning. Shall we forego saying Kaddish without the requisite minyan, for example? Some of our decisions may cause others, especially family and friends, to be uncomfortable, and they may offer their opinions even when we don't ask them for advice. Our first instinct may be to simply reject their words. But during this month of introspective learning, we should choose to listen a little more attentively. There may indeed be something to learn from what they have to say, even if we don't care for how they choose to say it. As the prophets demonstrated in their reprimand of our ancestors, *tochekha*, rebuke, is required of all of us so that we may learn from the experience of our mistakes.

PERSONAL REFLECTIONS

_____

_____

_____

_____

_____

> *She weeps bitterly in the night*
> *And tears are on her cheeks.*
>
> —Lamentations 1:2

The thought of Jerusalem in ruins shadows nearly every Jewish celebration. According to Jewish law, synagogues are to be built with roughly hewn, unfinished cornerstones to remind us of the destruction of the ancient Temple in Jerusalem. Our mourning for Jerusalem is the reason for many Jewish customs, including the traditional prohibition of some musical instruments on Shabbat, for they express joy and were used in the Temple. It is not surprising, therefore, that from the very beginning of our personal mourning, we include references to those among us who mourn for Jerusalem. This illustrates the common bond that we all share even though our personal experience of mourning is unique. We are all mourners. And just as we will eventually emerge from mourning Jerusalem—when the weeping will stop—we will eventually emerge from our personal state of mourning, having learned a great deal about ourselves along the way.

PERSONAL REFLECTIONS

_____

_____

_____

_____

Wednesday/Yom Revii _____ (today's date)

Surely business turns a wise person into a fool.
—Ecclesiastes 7:7

$\mathcal{T}$his is one of the many insights that Ecclesiastes had about life. A comment by a rabbi who lived many years later helps us understand Ecclesiastes' words. During the mourning process, we often drown ourselves in our work. This lets us busy ourselves so that we do not have to dwell on our own sadness. But take heed: "When a wise person busies himself [or herself] with many matters, his [or her] wisdom becomes confused" (*Exodus Rabbah* 6:2). We still have much to learn about life.

PERSONAL REFLECTIONS

_____

_____

_____

_____

_____

_____

Thursday/Yom Chamishi _____ (today's date)

Adonai, You have examined me and know me.
—Psalm 139:1

*T*his psalm, perhaps more than any other, is an admission by the writer of Psalms that it takes time to dig beneath the deep recesses of the soul. The Psalmist learned from personal experience that it often takes the mourner these five months to learn important things about the self. Moreover, we learn the important questions to ask, and we develop the courage to ask them. If we live a life that reflects the covenant we share with God, we find that we can open ourselves to God in ways that we have not been able to do with any human being. This is especially comforting when we may have shared so much of our self so openly with the deceased. Now, only God is prepared to listen.

PERSONAL REFLECTIONS

_____

_____

_____

_____

_____

_____

Friday/Yom Shishi _____ (today's date)

> *And Moses went down from the mount*
> *to the people.*
>
> —Exodus 19:14

*A*fter personally preparing for the task, Moses ascended Mount Sinai in order to encounter God and receive the Torah revelation on behalf of the Jewish people. He remained on the summit for 40 days (a numerical idiom in the Bible that usually reflects a special measure of sacred time). During that period, Moses reflected on his own strengths and weaknesses, as well as on his ability to lead the people. Had he not taken the time to reflect on himself, he may not have known that he had to go down the mountain in order to again meet the people. Revelation inspired his leadership. On the mountain, Moses encountered God. When he descended the mountain, he realized that he had to be with the people to discover his essential self.

PERSONAL REFLECTIONS

_____

_____

_____

_____

_____

_____

[Jacob] wrestled with an angel and prevailed;
he cried out and entreated him,
who met him at Bet El
and there spoke to us.

—Hosea 12:5

*T*he prophet Hosea ponders a well-known story from Genesis: Jacob camps for the night and encounters God during his slumber. Some say that Jacob wrestled with an angel. Others suggest that he wrestled with the dark side of himself (what is also called the *yetzer harah*, the inclination to do evil). Whenever we look at ourselves with soul-piercing honesty, we encounter our dark side. But Hosea reminds us that Jacob prevailed, just as we will emerge intact during this period of mourning. In the midst of Jacob's encounter, God spoke to him. And after the encounter, he emerged as a new person because he was spiritually energized from the experience. He grew from Jacob to become Israel. We can do the same.

PERSONAL REFLECTIONS

_____

_____

_____

_____

_____

A Meditation
Before Saying Kaddish

⚬〜〜⚬

In this moment of silence, a still, small voice speaks in the depths of my spirit. It speaks to me of all that I must do to come closer to God and grow in God's likeness. I must work with untiring faithfulness, even when no one's eye is upon me. I must come to the end of each day with a feeling that I used its gifts wisely and faced its trials courageously. I must try to judge others less harshly and love them more freely. I must be loyal to my people and heritage, seeking greater knowledge of our tradition and putting its teaching to work in my life. May I become ever more conscious to my dignity as a human being, and may I learn to see the divinity in every person I meet. Then, indeed, shall I come closer to God and grow in God's likeness.

—*Adapted by* RABBI BENNETT MILLER

Self-Reflection

> *Take Joshua, the son of Nun,*
> *a person in whom is spirit.*
>
> —Numbers 27:18

*A*s Moses prepared to relinquish his leadership of the Israelites (since he was prohibited from crossing the Jordan
River with them), he had to choose a successor. This is
something that we are not always privileged to do. Joshua
was chosen because of his spiritual optimism. He saw the
potential for holiness inherent in the Promised Land even
when his fellow scouts—who were sent ahead to evaluate
Canaan—saw only danger and certain destruction. The Israelites had left Egypt and wandered the desert. Like some
of us, many of them were afraid of the future as it lay directly ahead of them. Moses teaches us something that we
also learn once again during this month in the process of
our mourning: Our beloved deceased had to let go and let
others grow beyond him or her.

PERSONAL REFLECTIONS

_____

_____

_____

_____

_____

When I sit down or stand up, You know me.
You discern my thoughts from afar.

—Psalm 139:2

*A*s the middle of this year of mourning unfolds, friends and relatives have focused on their own lives. We may get together with them for holidays or special occasions, but it is unrealistic to expect them to attend to our needs now as much as they did in the earlier days of our mourning. This may disappoint or even hurt us. We may spend more time by ourselves, wrapped in the cocoon of personal thoughts and memories. This can lead us to probe the self more deeply with each passing day. We may think that we are alone, but we are not. Listen to the words of the Psalmist, who feels the presence of God wherever life's journey takes her.

PERSONAL REFLECTIONS

Tuesday/Yom Shelishi _____ (today's date)

> *You observe my walking and reclining*
> *and are familiar with all my ways.*
>
> —Psalm 139:3

*T*oday's *kavannah*, a verse selected to focus our thoughts, is intentionally taken from the same psalm that was included in yesterday's entry. It frames the entire month of mourning, just as our tradition suggests reading a specific psalm for individual days of the week or holidays. This psalm continues from the day before just as our feelings do not always change from the previous day. Likewise, the presence of God in our life, as the Psalmist notes, remains constant from day to day—but only if we acknowledge this. Even if we did not have an intimate relationship with God before our loved one died, mourning encourages and nurtures it, just when we need it most.

PERSONAL REFLECTIONS

_____

_____

_____

_____

_____

_____

_____

Wednesday/Yom Revii _____ (today's date)

> *There is not a word on my tongue*
> *but that You, Adonai, know it well.*
> —Psalm 139:4

*W*e say many things to many people during mourning. Some words we regret as soon as we utter them. As one rabbi suggested as an image for the challenge of repentance prior to Yom Kippur, it is as if we open a feather pillow to the wind and then try to collect them once again. In time, perhaps as we approach Yom Kippur, we will find the strength to ask others to forgive us for what we have said, although most people will not understand the pain that precipitated our words. Golda Meir once said that the state of mourning allows people to say whatever they want. Whether they are words that are said or even thoughts that are never given voice, God hears our pain and forgives us. We must forgive ourselves, as well.

PERSONAL REFLECTIONS

_____

_____

_____

_____

_____

Thursday/Yom Chamishi _____ (today's date)

Blessed is the One who discerns secrets.
—Babylonian Talmud, *Berakhot* 58a

The rabbis teach us to say 100 blessings each day. This is not a passive obligation. Instead, we are encouraged to find reasons in the world to offer blessing. These mitzvot, or Divine instructions, are particularly important to do during mourning. According to the Talmud, "This blessing is to be said when you see a large number of Jewish people, for the mind of each of them is not like the mind of any other, nor is the countenance of each of them like the countenance of any other" (*Berakhot* 58a). As we say this blessing, we recognize God as the Source of all blessings. God reveals to us that secret gift that everyone possesses. That includes each of us, too.

PERSONAL REFLECTIONS

_____

_____

_____

_____

_____

_____

_____

> *Take this book of Torah.*
> —Deuteronomy 31:26

*E*ven among those who believe that God dictated the entire Torah word for word to Moses on the top of Mount Sinai, there is a great deal of controversy regarding the end of Deuteronomy. How is it possible that Moses wrote about the end of his own life? According to the rabbis, Moses wrote the words as God dictated them on top of Sinai. Yet, in the face of his own mortality—one of the major life issues that is also forced upon us as we mourn for another—Moses realized that he still had important work to do. So prior to his death, Moses gave the Torah to Joshua and told him to lead the people forward. As we see our life unfolding in front of us, we must share the Torah of our lives with others.

PERSONAL REFLECTIONS

_____

_____

_____

_____

_____

_____

_____

Saturday/Shabbat _____ (today's date)

For behold, I will save you from that distant place,
and your offspring from the land of your captivity;
Jacob shall return; and be tranquil and
none shall make you afraid.
—Jeremiah 46:27b–28a

This prophetic text is read alongside the Torah's telling of the story of Pharaoh in the Book of Exodus. While it reflects the period of slavery in Egypt, it offers comfort to the Israelites who were exiled to Babylonia following the destruction of the Temple in Jerusalem. During mourning, we may feel exiled and estranged; this feeling may intensify as we look more deeply into ourselves. That's why the words above are so important to be read in the context of the serenity that Shabbat offers. Jeremiah's prophecy will come true: We *will* be redeemed from the distant place we now occupy and brought back to the land of promise. And no one will make us afraid. God will make sure of that.

PERSONAL REFLECTIONS

_____

_____

_____

_____

_____

A Meditation
Before Saying Kaddish

ↄ๛๛ഒ

The death of those close to our hearts grieves and humbles us. It devastates our lives, lives that once were filled with the warmth of their presence. It reminds us that we all must die, even the most humble and righteous among us. And yet we know that life does not end at the grave; the soul lives on. How, then, do we accept the reality of death? By remembering the goodness of our loved ones and by shaping our lives after their example. For the memory of the righteous is truly a blessing, an inspiration for all our days. May our lives be worthy of their memory, always.

—*VETAHER LIBENU*

SEVEN

Feeling Isolated and Alone

Adonai is my Shepherd,
I lack nothing.
—Psalm 23:1*

ᏙᎻᎪᎾ

Throughout the year of mourning, we each grieve in our own personal way. During the early days of mourning, even though we were buoyed by the surrounding support of friends and relatives, we still felt isolated and alone. We may also have a deep resentment at being left alone by the deceased to face the challenges of life. For as much comfort as community brings, ultimately we still mourn alone. As the first year of our bereavement continues, we may feel an even greater sense of isolation from others. This can lead to despair. And the despair may lead to greater isolation. Rabbi Emanuel Feldman, editor of *Tradition* magazine, summarized the mourner's isolation this way: "I do not exist. I am not I. I am an alien in the land of the living." The Jewish sacred resources that we

---

*The Twenty-third Psalm is generally read by mourners.

bring to mourning help break this cycle of isolation and despair before it does irreparable damage to our spirit.

Recognizing our tendency toward feeling isolated during this phase of our mourning, we have to work harder to maintain our relationships with the community. Hillel said it best: "Do not separate yourself from the community." This is not easy because the structure of many of our daily activities does not allow for it. That is one of the reasons we seek out community in order to say Kaddish in its midst.

Maintaining a connection to Jewish sources helps us stay connected with the Jewish community in a way that transcends space and time. Matriarchs and patriarchs, prophets and sages, all become part of our inner sanctum as we invite them into dialogue. This helps alleviate our feelings of alienation and isolation. Above all, we have to constantly remind ourselves of one thing: We are never alone as long as we invite God into our lives.

Isolation

Sunday/Yom Rishon _____ (today's date)

> *Jacob was left alone. Then some man wrestled*
> *with him until the break of dawn.*
>
> —Genesis 32:25

*J*acob discovered something during his nighttime encounter that we are forced to learn during the many days of our mourning. Even though we want to be surrounded by people who offer us comfort, Jacob, like us, was not able to learn this bit of Torah until after he was left alone. There seemed to be too much dissonance in his life for him to realize it before his nocturnal wrestling: too many people, too much noise. It took that lonely, frightening excursion for him to learn that even when we may think that we are alone, we are, in fact, never alone. Jacob tarried for the night, thinking that he was only settling down for slumber. Little did Jacob know that when he stopped for the night that he would encounter the Divine.

PERSONAL REFLECTIONS

_____

_____

_____

_____

_____

_____

> *The purpose of prayer is to leave us*
> *alone with God.*

—Rabbi Leo Baeck, *The Essence of Judaism*

*W*e often feel that we have been left alone in our mourning, isolated from other people and abandoned by God. Although many people will continue to support us along the way, particularly as we join them in a community minyan to pray, we still have to mourn alone. We may prefer not to face the unique loneliness of standing to say Kaddish. So why do we pray? In our prayers, we ask God for comfort and support. The prayer experience itself provides us with a great deal of solace. But there is more, for the purpose of prayer is to provide us with the opportunity to enter into an intimate relationship with the Divine. Seize this opportunity and pray so that you may know what we already have learned. May God always be at your side.

PERSONAL REFLECTIONS

_____

_____

_____

_____

_____

_____

> *The Gerer Rebbe taught, "Exile contains*
> *redemption within itself, as a seed contains the*
> *fruit. Right work and real diligence will bring out*
> *the hidden reward."*
> —*Siach Sifrei Kodesh* I, 13

It is hard to accept what the Gerer Rebbe, Rabbi Yehudah Aryeh Leib, a nineteenth-century Hasidic teacher, has to say while we are still mourning. But that is, indeed, why he is teaching it to us now. It seems like the loneliness and exile we feel will never end. As time passes, how can we, indeed, learn anything from the pain we feel? That's why we have to attend to the hard work of mourning. Through the mourning process, we learn to treasure the moments we have with those we love. We will also experience every living moment as a blessing from God, especially the everyday miracles of routine living that we previously took for granted. The hidden reward of this is that we might teach the Torah that we have learned to others.

PERSONAL REFLECTIONS

_____

_____

_____

_____

If a Jewish person chooses to remain distant from their people when in personal trouble, that individual's two angels put their hands over the person's head and say: "This one shall also be excluded from their consolation."

—Babylonian Talmud, *Taanit* 11a

*J*t takes a great deal of Divine attention to look after each of us. That is why the Talmud implies that God has sent two angels ("Divine messengers" as they are also called elsewhere in the Talmud) to look after the well-being of each person. This is particularly true during the entire period of mourning when we need God's care and concern perhaps more than any other time in our lives. But we do not have to remain alone in our mourning, as we may now feel that we do. The sages counsel us that while we mourn, we still have the obligation to reach out to others who also need our help. By doing so, we can encourage Divine consolation for all.

PERSONAL REFLECTIONS

_____

_____

_____

_____

_____

Thursday/Yom Chamishi _____ (today's date)

> *Prisoners cannot free themselves.*
> —Babylonian Talmud, *Berakhot* 5b

*T*his comment may seem odd for us to consider during mourning. However, the wisdom of the rabbis often glimmers deep inside the text and cannot be readily seen unless we are prepared to probe its depths. Some of us behave as if we were prisoners while mourning. We feel alone, unable to move forward with our lives. While the rituals for mourning conclude after the first year, we may prolong it, making ourselves into prisoners. When we act as if we are prisoners in our mourning, we are not able to free ourselves and move on with our healing and our lives.

PERSONAL REFLECTIONS

_____

_____

_____

_____

_____

_____

_____

_____

Friday/Yom Shishi   _____ (today's date)

> *I will send a faintness into their heart in the lands*
> *of their enemies; the sound of a driven leaf shall*
> *chase them; they shall flee . . . And fall when*
> *none pursues.*
>
> —Leviticus 26:36

This section of Leviticus aptly describes a multitude of feelings, all common to mourning. When we feel isolated and alone—frequent feelings we now experience—we may be frightened by many things, particularly at night: An unfamiliar house noise. A siren piercing the stillness of the night. People talking outside our living room window. Even "the sound of a driven leaf" may cause us panic. And we may feel as if we do not have the strength to face our fears. As we come to understand the power of the Divine in our lives, however, these noises will no longer cause us any concern. Instead, we will welcome them as the sounds of life that penetrate the darkness.

PERSONAL REFLECTIONS

_____

_____

_____

_____

_____

_____

[Oh] human, stand on your own feet and I will
speak to you.

—Ezekiel 2:1

*I*t sounds rather banal, but so do many things that are essentially true. During mourning, we may find it difficult to stand on our own feet. We may tire easily and grow weary. As a result, we continue to need the support of others. We are assured through the prophet Ezekiel that, as difficult as it seems, we will regain that ability to stand erect. On Shabbat, we are given a sense of where that strength comes from: the Holy One of Blessing. The extra soul that God sends our way to strengthen us during Shabbat helps to refresh and renew us for the week ahead and the work we have yet to do.

PERSONAL REFLECTIONS

_____

_____

_____

_____

_____

_____

A Meditation Before Saying Kaddish

⟨∞⟩

By requiring that the Kaddish be recited with a quorum of worshipers, Judaism renders the mourner a profound service. A minyan almost invariably includes other mourners and thus brings home the realization that we alone have not been singled out.

The burning question, "Why did God do this to me?," loses much of its sting when others also rise to recite the Kaddish. We are not lonely travelers in the valley of the shadow. We thus see death for what it is—not a malevolent act of a vindictive God, but part of the incomprehensible mystery of human existence in which light and dark, joy and sadness, birth and death are interwoven and inseparable.

—RABBI SIDNEY GREENBERG

Estrangement

Sunday/Yom Rishon _____ (today's date)

> *Thus Israel dwells in safety alone,*
> *Untroubled is Jacob's abode,*
> *In a land of grain and wine*
> *Under heavens dripping dew.*
>
> —Deuteronomy 33:28

*T*his verse is taken from Moses' farewell speech to the people as they prepare to depart for Canaan without him. It is not part of the regular cycle of weekly Torah readings. Instead, it is read each year only on Simchat Torah. The Torah speaks of the loneliness that Moses feels because he cannot accompany the Jewish people any longer. Sometimes we think of solitude as a means of bringing solace to the soul. Often, we consider it a function of loneliness or isolation that may threaten our personal security. In the midst of our joyous celebration of Torah on Simchat Torah, we are taught something completely different: Even when Israel, individually or collectively, is alone, she dwells in safety. Moreover, she will be blessed. And so will you.

PERSONAL REFLECTIONS

_____

_____

_____

_____

I have none but myself to depend on.
—Babylonian Talmud, *Avodah Zarah* 17a

*I*n this statement from *Avodah Zarah*, the rabbis of the Talmud express a feeling that we often experience, particularly during this period of mourning. Because these rabbis often suffered that feeling as a result of their own life's journey, they evolved the idea of minyan (prayer quorum) and fashioned it as part of the essential fabric of the Jewish community: a minimum of ten people gathered together for prayer and mutual support. Whether or not we are mourning, we may feel alone. But as members of the minyan—previously just a group of unrelated individuals—join their voice to ours, that sense of estrangement is diminished. As we affirm each word of Kaddish as part of a new community, feelings of isolation vanish from our midst.

PERSONAL REFLECTIONS

_____

_____

_____

_____

_____

_____

Do not separate yourself from your community.
—*Pirke Avot* 2:4

*T*his passage from *Pirke Avot* sounds like good advice, particularly as we mourn. We need the support of others, but it isn't always that simple. Without the one we lost, we may not feel as comfortable in the synagogue community that we used to call our own. We may even feel isolated and estranged. That's why the rabbis offer us the above advice: They know full well that it will take a great deal of extra work for us to maintain our ties with the community. But they are not asking us to do it alone; we are all in this together, for, as the rabbis say, all of the people of Israel are responsible for each other.

PERSONAL REFLECTIONS

_____

_____

_____

_____

_____

_____

_____

*Join a community by which alone your work can
be made universal and eternal in its results.*
—Samson Raphael Hirsch, *Nineteen Letters*

*I*f you have not already reestablished ties with your community, now is the time. This is an indispensable part of the mourning process. Some connections to the community may have loosened during past months. A strong sense of affiliation will probably not evolve overnight. As you find your way back to the community, some people may feel uncomfortable being with you because of your loss. They won't know what to say or do. So it is time to seek out a community that makes you comfortable. Only such a community will help you realize the insight contained in Rabbi Hirsch's words above. In the midst of that community, you will find comfort.

PERSONAL REFLECTIONS

_____

_____

_____

_____

_____

_____

_____

*The wicked child is the one who acts to become
separate from the community.*
—*Mekhilta* to Exodus 13:8

*T*his idea comes from the Passover story about the four children that is related in the Haggadah: One was wise, one was wicked, one was uncomplicated, and one was too young to understand the transformative nature of the Exodus experience. While we tell the story of the Exodus so that everyone may hear it, even those among us who know the details of the story are instructed to listen so that we may be reminded of God's role in our personal redemption from slavery. These four children reflect different attitudes that might be expressed regarding the Exodus. The rabbis call one child "wicked" because he separated himself from the community. Had others done so in Egypt, they may not have been redeemed. Stay connected to community. Your future life depends on it.

PERSONAL REFLECTIONS

_____

_____

_____

_____

_____

_____

I give the land you sojourn in to you and your
offspring to come, the entire land of Canaan, as
an everlasting possession. I will be their God.
—Genesis 17:8

This statement from Genesis comes from the exquisite selection known as *Lekh Lekha* and includes God's call to Abraham. This promise that God made to him extends throughout the generations and reaches us this day. But the most important aspect of the promise has nothing to do with the acquisition or possession of the land. Instead, it is this final part of the statement that God makes to Abraham that is significant to us in our mourning: "I will be their God." In other words, no matter how isolated and alone you feel in your journey to the Promised Land or anywhere else in your life, God will always be with you and with those who come after you. What more could any person ask for themselves or for their children?

PERSONAL REFLECTIONS

_____

_____

_____

_____

_____

_____

Saturday/Shabbat _____ (today's date)

> *The house of Israel went into captivity . . .*
> *because they broke faith with Me.*
>
> —Ezekiel 39:23

Ezekiel is one of the prophets who speaks from the midst of exile. Traditional commentators read this history of the Jewish people in a particular way: We were expelled from Jerusalem because we broke the covenant established with God on Sinai. The exile included captivity during which we lost the precious opportunity to direct our own lives. We were forced to endure this servitude so we could learn from our experience. While the exile was real for our ancestors, it remains a symbol for us. When we lose our faith in God, we may as well be in exile, captives of another nation. We cannot afford to break our faith with God while we mourn. Then we might truly find ourselves alone and in exile.

PERSONAL REFLECTIONS

_____

_____

_____

_____

_____

_____

A Meditation Before Saying Kaddish

Jews have learned not to be afraid of mourning, perhaps because Jewish history is a continuous cycle of grief and rebirth, death and renewal. The Kaddish prayer helps us to understand this cycle.

Saying Kaddish helps me reconcile being a fatherless child with being a human who strives for a spiritual relationship with God. Sometimes when I am davening, I'll squeeze the leather tefillin strap in my left hand. I feel like I am squeezing God's hand. God is there with me and I'm not alone.

—PHYLLIS TOBACK

Detachment

Sunday/Yom Rishon _____ (today's date)

> *The stranger living with you must be treated like*
> *the native. Love that person just like yourself, for*
> *you were strangers in the land of Egypt. I am*
> *Adonai your God.*
>
> —Leviticus 19:34

*W*hile this statement from Leviticus evolved from when our people were slaves in Egypt, it has become a complement to the Jewish journey through history. Feeling alienated and alone, our experience as outsiders has taught us to reach out to others. As mourners, we easily recall the experience from our people's collective past. As you mourn, you will meet other mourners who have recently begun to grieve. They are experiencing feelings that you first encountered some months ago. Martin Buber, the philosopher/theologian, argued that we experience God in the relationship we develop with others. Hence, the statement of today's verse: "Love that person just like yourself. . . ." When you treat others as if they were you, the way you want to be treated, you invite God's presence to dwell in your midst.

PERSONAL REFLECTIONS

_____

_____

_____

_____

Exile atones for everything.
—Babylonian Talmud, *Sanhedrin* 37b

*I*t is hard to accept this teaching of the rabbis on an initial reading. Therefore, we must probe its depth to understand its message. Only when we do not find meaning in what we are forced to endure may our travails be called "suffering." Perhaps that is what the rabbis had in mind when they wrote down this teaching. Like mourning, our experience of being separated from someone we love is similar to feeling like our people did in exile. Now we are forced to consider many things, some of which we may not have contemplated otherwise: deeds we have done, persons we have wronged, actions we should have avoided. And now during mourning, we face them all alone. So in the exile-like stage of our mourning, we may indeed be in a position to atone for many things. Other things will have to wait for Yom Kippur.

PERSONAL REFLECTIONS

_____

_____

_____

_____

_____

_____

*As long as Israel is in exile, the Divine Name
is incomplete.*

—*Zohar* I, 154b–155a

It may not always seem that way, but God suffers nearly as much as we do, even if on a different scale. This is part of our relationship with the Divine that continually evolves, matures, and grows. And when mourning forces isolation on us, we feel detached from our community. As the Zohar suggests, isolation and exile challenge God's Name. We must do our work in the world, but God has a Divine reputation to uphold. And we are obliged to have God uphold it. What we learned while in exile from Israel, we can apply to our mourning. May whatever we do to honor the memory of the deceased help complete the Divine Name and bring God near to us.

PERSONAL REFLECTIONS

_____

_____

_____

_____

_____

_____

When the way is long, company is pleasant.
—Babylonian Talmud, *Sukkah* 52a

Nobody has to explain to you what the rabbis were teaching in this statement from the Talmud. The way of mourning is, indeed, long and lonely nearly every step along the way. But Judaism is found in the midst of community. That's why we are required to say Kaddish in the context of a minyan (the ten-member prayer quorum). Our identity as a people was forged as we traveled as a community 600,000-strong through the desert. We confronted the challenges of the desert as a people. The rabbis' guidance about the value of others reminds members of the community to join you on your way toward healing and wholeness. When they choose to join you, open yourselves up to them as they have opened their hearts to you.

PERSONAL REFLECTIONS

_____

_____

_____

_____

_____

_____

Thursday/Yom Chamishi _____ (today's date)

Oh that I had the wings of a dove. I would fly
away and be at rest.

—Psalm 55:7

The dove is a special bird, a symbol of all that is good in the world. She is gentle and refuses to defend herself even when threatened. Noah sent one out after the Flood. And she became a symbol of peace and tranquillity for us and for the world. The dove idealizes the world, seeing it as she would like it to be. However unrealistic it is, there are many times we would like to escape reality. This is particularly true regarding our present state of mourning. In doing so, we might find rest elsewhere. But, just as we find ourselves now, we would still be alone. And our loved one would still be gone. So consider your loneliness to be a restorative solitude. And in it, may you find some rest.

PERSONAL REFLECTIONS

_____

_____

_____

_____

_____

_____

_____

It is holy (kadosh) *to you.*

—Exodus 31:14

*E*ach week, we prepare for Shabbat. Some people spend several days in preparation. As sunset on Friday casts its glow on us, we are swept into a time that is both paradise past and messianic future. It is ironic that on Shabbat, generally a time for family and the time of Israel's joy which brings us closer to God, we feel more than any other time that we are alone. But as we remember the covenant between Israel and God, we remind ourselves that we are never alone. This covenant, sealed on Sinai thousands of years ago, is uniquely represented by Shabbat which is holy. In Hebrew, holy (*kadosh*) also means separate, distinct, alone. Like Shabbat, the time we spend alone can be holy, if we can elevate it heavenward.

PERSONAL REFLECTIONS

_____

_____

_____

_____

_____

> *Pack your bags for exile,*
> *Daughter of Egypt, dwelling so safe and sound!*
> *Memphis will become a desolation,*
> *an uninhabited ruin!*
>
> —Jeremiah 46:19

In the midst of his warning to Israel, Jeremiah cautions those who have taken the Israelites captive and sent them from the land: They may appear victorious now, but they will soon be among the defeated. Although the Israelites may appear to have forever lost the land, Israel will return from her exile at the end of this captivity. She will be at home once again. That promise is ours. While we may feel isolated and alone as a result of our mourning—and even blame God for forcing it upon us—at the end of this mourning process, we will return from our exile. In exile, Israel was able to consider her deeds and bring direction to her future. We can do the same.

PERSONAL REFLECTIONS

_____

_____

_____

_____

_____

A Meditation
Before Saying Kaddish

⟨~⟩

God cares for each individual life. When God's soldiers die, God mourns, as it were, each person. When a person dies, God's own Name is diminished, God's own sanctity lessened. God's Kingdom experiences a terrible vacancy. God suffers, as it were, just as the human mourner suffers.

When we recite Kaddish, we offer God consolation for this loss. We say *Yitgadal*: Your name has been diminished; may it be magnified. *Yitkadash*: Your sanctity has been lessened; may it be increased. *Yamlikh malkhutai*: Your kingdom has suffered a sudden loss; may it reign eternally.

Before reciting the Kaddish, let us reflect on our loss and the Source of all growth and goodness. Let us reflect on praising God, who stands beside us as a mourner and who also is the Promise on which we build tomorrow.

—S. Y. AGNON, *as retold by Rabbi Thomas Louchheim*

Separation

Sunday/Yom Rishon _____ (today's date)

Do not hate your brother in your heart.
—Leviticus 19:17

*A*s we near the completion of this seventh month of mourning and we reestablish our way in the world, we may be tempted to feel angry with those around us whose lives seem not to have been touched by mourning. However, we must remember that there is no one who does not eventually face the death of someone they love. This is a high price for the blessings of life, but it is the one we must pay for love. The Torah supports our grief by reminding us: Do not hate your brother and sister. As we might expect, the Torah is teaching us a more important lesson: Those we might be tempted to hate *are* our brothers and sisters.

PERSONAL REFLECTIONS

_____

_____

_____

_____

_____

Monday/Yom Sheni _____ (today's date)

*Drink water out of your own cistern and running
water out of your own well.*

—Proverbs 5:15

Each passage in the Book of Proverbs challenges us to probe deeply to find its profound meaning. Because each individual proverb often sounds like a simple truism, we may overlook its wisdom. But insights such as the one contained in this verse from Proverbs help us achieve self-reliance. In mourning, we have learned to rely on ourselves in ways that we may not have previously thought possible. There is no choice. Supported by God, when we find ourselves alone, we gather the inner strength necessary to move forward. The waters that the writer of Proverbs mentions reflect the waters of our personal redemption. Come let us drink them together so that we may gain strength for our mourning.

PERSONAL REFLECTIONS

_____

_____

_____

_____

_____

_____

Nothing that I have is important to me for this world is not mine.

—*Derech Eretz* 1:1

*B*y spending time alone in our thoughts, we are able to consider certain truths, the kind the rabbis have suggested for many centuries. However, we may not have been ready to learn them until this phase of our mourning. Now many of the words of our own prayers, culled from the yearnings of our people, may have become ardent principles for our daily living. Earthly possessions diminish in value as we consider them against the trajectory of time. They are of no lasting value to us or to those whom we will leave behind. Instead, we seek to discover the eternal values that guide our lives, for they provide a foundation on which future generations may grow and through which we may continue to live.

PERSONAL REFLECTIONS

_____

_____

_____

_____

_____

_____

Silence is a fence for wisdom.

—*Pirke Avot* 3:13

*T*he rabbis frequently employ the image of a fence to clarify their abstract teachings. We know that a fence may keep things corralled, unable to leave their confines. We also know, on the other hand, that a fence may offer protection from intruders. Fences also offer us privacy. When we are alone as a result of our mourning, we may find a measure of comfort in silence. Rebbe Nachman of Breslov actually taught us the wisdom of the "silent scream." He advised us to express ourselves from the depths of our souls and yell as loudly as possible without emitting a sound. We can also use this silent time to walk, to study, to think. Within the limits of our silence, we may also find wisdom. Life itself is perhaps the greatest teacher of wisdom. And that wisdom is our own fence.

PERSONAL REFLECTIONS

_____

_____

_____

_____

_____

_____

Woe to the one who is alone when falling.
—Ecclesiastes 4:10

*E*cclesiastes gained wisdom from living a life rich with a variety of experience. Offering us insight from personal encounters with daily living, he knows how it feels to be alone. We understand that mourning forces us to be alone. And that is painful. According to Ecclesiastes, there seems to be no alternative to solitude at such times. But being alone also can offer us new opportunities to gain wisdom and insight from the surrounding world. We can reach out to others and learn from them. They may be uncomfortable in reaching out to us on their own. But they will respond to our invitation. It is part of the system of spiritual logic: When we reach out to others, we can help ourselves. Likewise, others help themselves by helping us!

PERSONAL REFLECTIONS

_____

_____

_____

_____

_____

_____

Friday/Yom Shishi _____ (today's date)

You are all standing here this day.
—Deuteronomy 29:9

*A*fter months of wandering, we stood at the foot of Sinai, 600,000 trembling people waiting to receive God's revelation through the word of Moses. Fearful and tired, we longed to hear the comfort of God's voice. Just as we have felt throughout our mourning, we felt alone in the midst of community. Yet, we stood together as one people. Through all of the challenges that we have now faced, personally and collectively, we still stand as that people who journeyed through the desert on the way to the Promised Land: those who are with us today, those who are no longer with us, and those who are yet unborn.

PERSONAL REFLECTIONS

_____

_____

_____

_____

_____

_____

_____

Saturday/Shabbat _____ (today's date)

> *Return, O Israel, to Adonai your God, for you*
> *have stumbled in your iniquity. Take words [of*
> *Torah] with you and return to Adonai and say:*
> *"Forgive all iniquity and accept the good; and we*
> *will offer the fruit of our lips."*
>
> —Hosea 14:2–3

*T*his is one of my favorite texts from the haftarot and from the entire collection of prophetic literature. I use it to calm myself, particularly when I am distressed and alone, particularly on Shabbat even when I am in the synagogue and surrounded by a large group of people. Even then, I sometimes still feel alone. I fully recognize that I have "stumbled in my iniquity" and must repair any damage I caused. I also have to find a way to open myself to God so that I can forgive myself. I recognize that it is only possible by applying the healing balm of Torah. And so I take these words with me and return to God. During mourning, when you feel isolated and alone, you can do the same.

PERSONAL REFLECTIONS

_____

_____

_____

_____

A Meditation
Before Saying Kaddish

⌘

Say the old masters, "What is life like?" "Life," said they, "is like a musical instrument." God plays upon the instrument. The time may come when the instrument that had felt the touch of the hand of God, and had responded to its caressing, may crumble and fall into dust. But they who have heard the melody will have its notes ring in their ears to their last day. Our beloved one was a musical instrument in the hands of God. Eagerly, faithfully, he answered with the melody of his life to the touch of God's hands. We know that mortal remains will go back to dust, but we have heard the melody.

—Rabbi Gerson B. Levi

EIGHT

Withdrawing from the Past

*"The dust returns to the earth as it was,
but the spirit returns to God who gave it."*
—Ecclesiastes 12:7

We can never fully break from the past or from those who were in it. But there comes a time when we have to find a way to separate from the past and stop living in it. The pain that memory brings does not stop, but in our own way, we work to become detached from it. The process of mourning in Judaism helps us do this. Our ability to accomplish this difficult challenge identifies this stage in our mourning and bereavement. At first, we are frightened, fearful that we might forget the deceased. We hesitate to let go. We are afraid that we might forget images and memories, powerful reminders of their continuing presence in our lives. We recognize that the past helped shape our present and brought us to this day. But the past is behind us, and we must continue each day to gather the strength to move forward.

We are a people who does not forget its past. We constantly relive it in order to keep it alive within us. The power of memory permeates Jewish civilization. We encounter it throughout the Jewish calendar year. Memory is part of the secret of our survival. Even our prayers contain regular references to past events. We constantly recall the journey through Sinai, from Egypt to the Promised Land. We recall the binding of Isaac and sacrifices at the ancient Temple. These past events provide the present with their sacred quality.

During mourning, our memories of the deceased merge with the collective memory of our people and thereby become sacred. Their ancestral status rises to join the matriarchs and patriarchs of our people, those who guided us and brought us to this day. In this way, the memories of the deceased do not fade. Instead, they are brought into the context of eternity and become part of our celebration of the past and our hope for the future.

Looking Forward

Sunday/Yom Rishon   _____ (today's date)

> *When you approach a town to attack it,*
> *you shall offer it peace.*
> —Deuteronomy 20:10

This text from Deuteronomy is one of many that shaped ancient Israel's conscience as it prepared to enter the Promised Land and conquer and settle it. It was the only way to take possession of the land that God promised to our ancestors. These instructions reminded the Israelites that as they faced difficult challenges, they had to remember what they learned during their journey in the desert: Peace—which is marked by wholeness and harmony—provides us with direction for our lives. This passage from Deuteronomy speaks primarily of peace between peoples. As mourners, we have been forced to struggle with the angel of death, a formidable foe. And now we seek to regain a sense of balance, of inner peace in our lives.

PERSONAL REFLECTIONS

_____

_____

_____

_____

_____

> *For the miracles, and for the wonders . . . done*
> *for our ancestors in days past.*
> —From the additional prayer for the *Amidah*
> said during festivals

As we consider the past and our many months of mourning, we tend to feel melancholy and somewhat resentful that we have been forced to take on the role of mourner. Even as we enter this eighth month of mourning, these emotions still come and go unexpectedly. This will continue as we slowly face the full reality that our loved one has died. As difficult as it may seem, with this acknowledgment must come gratitude, an expression of thanks for the times shared, for the love expressed, and for the many memories that remain as we regain a sense of direction for our lives. Life itself is a miracle. And love is a wonder. We thank You, God, for life—and for love.

PERSONAL REFLECTIONS

_____

_____

_____

_____

_____

_____

When the Israelites sinned in the desert, Moses
offered up many prayers to God, but they were
not answered. However, when he said to God,
"Remember Abraham," an answer came.
—Babylonian Talmud, *Shabbat* 30

*W*e would expect Moses' prayers to God to be immediately answered as a result of the intimate relationship they shared. Although Moses was unlike any other prophet in Jewish history, in some ways he was just like us. This talmudic passage addresses the rabbinic concept of *zekhut avot*, the merit of our ancestors. Its insightful notion suggests that while we may not deserve God's attention, we receive it anyway because of the accrued merit of those who have come before us. These often include our deceased. We also gain *zekhut avot* through the very act of mourning, but when we continue the good works that our deceased left behind for us to do, we contribute to *zekhut avot* for those who come after us.

PERSONAL REFLECTIONS

_____

_____

_____

_____

_____

Wednesday/Yom Revii   _____ (today's date)

> *Adam's dust was gathered from all parts*
> *of the world.*
> —Babylonian Talmud, *Sanhedrin* 38

*T*his text is usually understood to explain the human creation story that is detailed in the early chapters of Genesis. The rabbis of the midrash suggest that the process of creation that God used emphasized that the entire human race evolved out of the same primordial human: Adam. The logic suggests that since we all have the same ancestor, then we are all equal. As a result, no one can claim superiority over another. But there is more to this talmudic lesson that is particularly relevant to our mourning. It teaches that the process of life and death is cyclic. Adam came from dust and returned to it, to the part of the world we call our own. As do we all.

PERSONAL REFLECTIONS

_____

_____

_____

_____

_____

_____

_____

Counsel in the heart of a human is like deep water, but an individual of understanding will draw it out.

—Proverbs 20:5

*M*any of our friends and neighbors may still want to give us counsel and advice. We may be tired of listening to them and want to be alone, yet there may be certain truths in what they say. If we take the time to listen and reflect deeply on their words, we will realize many things: We are still alive with life ahead of us. Others still depend on us. Listening for such advice can motivate us to move forward and loosen our grip on the past. We don't have to let go entirely, but we must commit ourselves to continue to reconstruct our lives, since the future cannot be built until we build a foundation for it out of the past.

PERSONAL REFLECTIONS

_____

_____

_____

_____

_____

_____

_____

God separated the light from the darkness.

—Genesis 1:4

*A*ccording to the biblical account of creation as masterfully told in Genesis, darkness and chaos existed before the creation of the world. Darkness came first, and then God dispelled the darkness by creating light. This Divine light illuminated the world throughout the evolving process of creation. We understand this sequence of events because it reflects our experience with mourning: Darkness, then light. Confusion, then resolution. Like creation, which occurred one day at a time and eventually established the world on its course, now our lives will also be set on their course. But the Torah wants to teach us another truth, one that will help us find strength during the process of mourning and beyond: God's light brings us out of the darkness and illumines our path in life.

PERSONAL REFLECTIONS

_____

_____

_____

_____

_____

_____

Saturday/Shabbat _____ (today's date)

> *They cried with a loud voice to Adonai,*
> *their God.*
>
> —Nehemiah 9:4

*A*s might be expected, the ancient Israelites cried out to God in the midst of their exile. They remembered their lives as they were in ancient Israel and longed to return. Eventually many of them did return. Others remained dispersed in lands throughout the world. When our ancestors returned to the land of Israel, it had changed, and during the exile, so had they. After many months of mourning, we now long to return to our normal routine, to a past with which we had become familiar. But life never seems to work that way. As we have learned during mourning, we may return home once again, but when we get there we realize: The present has changed the past.

PERSONAL REFLECTIONS

_____

_____

_____

_____

_____

_____

_____

A Meditation
Before Saying Kaddish

⟡

Death can only take from us what might have been. It cannot take from us what has already been. It cannot rob us of our past. The days and years we shared, the common adventures and joys, the "little nameless acts of kindness and of love"—all these are part of the ineradicable record. Death has no dominion over them.

—RABBI SIDNEY GREENBERG

Advancement

Sunday/Yom Rishon _____ (today's date)

> *Teach them to your children. Recite them when*
> *you stay at home, when you lie down and when*
> *you get up.*
>
> —Deuteronomy 6:7

*T*his passage, originally in the Book of Deuteronomy and now incorporated in the *Shema*, reiterates our responsibilities in the covenant. In the *Shema*, it appears in the middle of the paragraph that follows the main statement, "Hear O Israel. . . ," and reminds us that one of our tasks is to teach our children. We can do so primarily by example, although we are also told elsewhere in this same paragraph of the *Shema* to constantly repeat the teachings of the Torah to our children. And so, as we mourn, we train our children in the rites and rituals of Jewish mourning practice. Like the *Shema*, this stage in our mourning teaches our children to learn lessons from the past so that together we might advance the future.

PERSONAL REFLECTIONS

_____

_____

_____

_____

_____

A generation goes and a generation comes,
but the earth stands forever.

—Ecclesiastes 1:4

*T*his is what Ecclesiastes observed during his life. Like us, he experienced love and loss. No matter where this teacher traveled or what he did, the above insight was never compromised. While our lives may not be filled with the same extraordinary experiences as was the life of Ecclesiastes, our experience in this particular aspect of life is the same. At first, Ecclesiastes' words seem somewhat bitter or, at least, melancholy. But they are neither. Ecclesiastes' lesson reflects Judaism's firm grip on a reality that sits on a reliable foundation. And this, in turn, gives us hope that is supported by a profound and immovable belief in God. For it is God who keeps the earth—of which Ecclesiastes speaks—in motion.

PERSONAL REFLECTIONS

_____

_____

_____

_____

_____

_____

Tuesday/Yom Shelishi _____ (today's date)

Do not ask, "Why were the former days better than these?" for it is not out of wisdom that you ask it.

—Ecclesiastes 7:10

*E*cclesiastes was a great observer of life. He reflected on many of his own experiences so that we might learn from him. As Ecclesiastes noted, we often mistakenly consider the past to be better than the present, but only when we have not achieved the wisdom to assess it fully. Judaism teaches that we should never sever our ties with the past, since the past provides us with the sacred bond of memory. But we cannot be free if we are bound by chains that secure us to it. When we live in the past, our strength to move forward wanes. In this current stage of mourning, we reconcile the past with the present so that we might gain the wisdom to grow forward.

PERSONAL REFLECTIONS

_____

_____

_____

_____

_____

_____

> *No individual can be instructed entirely without*
> *a link to the past.*
>
> —Ahad Haam

*N*ow that we are finally moving away from the past during this stage of mourning, Judaism also teaches us to maintain a firm hold on it. This may seem like a contradiction, but our tradition urges us to achieve this delicate balance. That's what the Zionist Ahad Haam was striving to communicate. As we find it, we may also regain a sense of balance in our lives. After all, it is the memory of the past that teaches us to honor our beloved deceased and to consciously remember him or her, along with the others of our people who have died, on specific holiday commemorations such as Yom Kippur, Sukkot, Pesach, and Shavuot. And so as we move more deeply into the present and detach ourselves more fully from the past, we strive to regain the memory of the past, as well.

PERSONAL REFLECTIONS

_____

_____

_____

_____

_____

_____

> *Today you feel up. Don't let yesterdays and*
> *tomorrows bring you down.*
> —Rebbe Nachman of Breslov, *The Empty Chair*

While they are colored by a profound wisdom that is nearly unparalleled, Rebbe Nachman's instructions are generally simple and straightforward. He understands the spiritual predicament in which we find ourselves as mourners. His insight reflects the ups and downs we feel during the entire process of mourning and what we will feel once the formal process is over. But his lesson offers us a particularly powerful insight this month. In our rush to let go of the past and the pain that it represents, we may be tempted to race into the future. In doing so, we may lose the present, as well. We have many ups and many downs ahead of us. They are part of the rhythm of life. So Rebbe Nachman suggests that we simply hold onto the present with a firm faith and an unrelenting confidence in God.

PERSONAL REFLECTIONS

_____

_____

_____

_____

_____

*Adonai will scatter you among the people. Only
a scant few of you shall be left among the nations
to which Adonai will drive you.*
—Deuteronomy 4:27

*J*ewish historians and theologians frequently write about the "remnant of Israel," about those who have been scattered around the globe yet still cling to their covenant with God. Although their faith has been severely tested, they remain faithful. Some believe that this dispersion was a punishment for breaking faith with God and no longer following God's instructions for our lives. Others contend—and I count myself among them—that this scattering forced Israel to interact with surrounding cultures so it could be a "light unto the nations." While the original dispersal of our people occurred in ancient days, it occurs in every generation. By participating in the Jewish rituals of mourning and bereavement, we renew our loyalty to this small, but fiercely committed holy nation of Israel. Although circumstances may challenge our faith, we remain devoted to its continuity. As survivors, we are the remnant—and we are the future.

PERSONAL REFLECTIONS

_____

_____

_____

Saturday/Shabbat _____ (today's date)

Do you seek great things for yourself?
Seek them not.

—Jeremiah 45:5

*C*ertainly, we have learned this simple truth over the last months: Like many other Jewish practices, the Jewish rituals of mourning and bereavement are rather specific. The prescribed rituals provide us with the opportunity to do what is appropriate to honor the memory of the deceased without worrying whether we have done enough. At the same time, they prevent us from "displaying" our righteous piety by doing too much. As we regain our balance in the present during this stage of mourning, Jeremiah's message comes to us as a warning: We mourn to honor the deceased—and not to honor ourselves.

PERSONAL REFLECTIONS

_____

_____

_____

_____

_____

_____

_____

A Meditation
Before Saying Kaddish

⟜⟜⟜

However short, however long the time given to those who are near to us, strength will be fashioned through the gratitude of our hearts for the blessing of life itself. When the days of life are short, shall we curse the moments of beauty for their brevity, or prize them that they came to us at all? When toll is taken in the middle years, shall we be bitter for lack of more, or wall our tears with thanksgiving for what has been? When the bridge of three-score and ten has been crossed, shall we be torn with argument for a longer term, or be grateful for the fullness of the granted time?

Our sages said that all things might be lost save one: the spirit of gratitude that is ever present in the heart of man. They further said that as long as thanksgiving lasts, the world will endure. The waters of sadness are deep, but they will never extinguish the spark of gratefulness that is fed by our inherent recognition of God's goodness toward us. Let us fan that spark into a flame that will guide us happily into the future.

—*Adapted from* RABBI JOSEPH I. WEISS

Embracing the Present

Sunday/Yom Rishon   _____ (today's date)

> *This shall be to you a law for all time:*
> *To make atonement for the Israelites for all*
> *their sins once a year.*
>
> —Leviticus 16:34a

*J*ewish tradition offers each individual an annual period of self-reflection and introspection. It begins in Elul (late August/early September) and ends with Yom Kippur (the day noted in the passage above from Leviticus). Forty days to embrace our past—and then to let go of it. Throughout the year, we are given additional opportunities to do the same, particularly at the beginning of each new Hebrew month. And each time we do, we find a way to make peace with our past and to embrace the present. As we near the completion of our mourning, we are prepared once again to repeat this pattern of embracing and letting go, for it contains the essence for self-evaluation and personal growth. We evaluate the past to gird ourselves for the future.

PERSONAL REFLECTIONS

_____

_____

_____

_____

_____

> *It is necessary to build a sanctuary within,*
> *brick by brick.*
> —Rabbi Jakob J. Petuchowski

*E*ver since the days of the Bible, we have built sanctuaries in which our people could worship. In the desert, we carried the Tabernacle with us. Then we built the Temple in Jerusalem. Wherever we lived, we built synagogues so that we could worship together and build our community of collective memory. Regardless of where we pray, many of us still choose to pray together with others who share a path in life similar to our own. Rabbi Petuchowski, my own teacher, taught that the synagogue we build in which to pray is only as good as the prayers we utter in the heart. These are the bricks of the sanctuary we build for ourselves. In mourning and throughout life, we build them both one brick at a time.

PERSONAL REFLECTIONS

_____

_____

_____

_____

_____

When wisdom enters an individual,
subtlety enters with it.
—Babylonian Talmud, *Sotah* 21b

The Talmud teaches us about the nuances of wisdom but does not seem to teach us how to achieve it. As we proceed through each day in the mourning process, we gain new insights on life and love. This discernment does not come in one fell swoop. Rabbi Akiva, a popular talmudic sage, suggested that wisdom was like a rock that was slowly worn away by a drop of water that constantly fell against it. Wisdom, like mourning, is a process. It unfolds over time. Slowly, we see subtle hints of our understanding about the passage of time, fleeting moments of penetrating insight into life, particularly this month as we strive to withdraw from the past and embrace the present.

PERSONAL REFLECTIONS

_____

_____

_____

_____

_____

_____

_____

An heir steps into the shoes of a parent.
—Babylonian Talmud, *Eruvin* 70b

For those who mourn a parent, one of the most difficult aspects of bereavement is in recognizing that they have assumed the role of the senior generation in a family. This is not an easy step for most people even if we thought that we wanted it our entire life. But it is a necessary step in separating from the past. Along with our grief, we have to reckon with the challenge of our own finitude. It is part of the cycle of life and death, of growth and decay. We become fully responsible for the generation behind us as we "step into the shoes of a parent." In doing so, we bring the world closer to the messianic era by doing the work that they started and by continuing our own.

PERSONAL REFLECTIONS

_____

_____

_____

_____

_____

_____

_____

Thursday/Yom Chamishi _____ (today's date)

> *The increment given by the Holy One*
> *exceeds the principal.*
>
> —*Genesis Rabbah* 61:4

*T*hroughout the process of mourning, we are frequently tempted to think about how unfair life seems to be. We think that we deserve more—and that we have been shortchanged. That may be true, and we boldly tell God exactly how we feel. But if we are brutally honest with ourselves during this stage of our mourning, we may finally be able to admit that we have been blessed with much more than we have deserved. Like everyone else, we have made mistakes. Sometimes we try to correct those mistakes. At other times, our errors may simply form the habit of our lives. It takes nearly a full year of mourning to realize that life is a gift given to us by God.

PERSONAL REFLECTIONS

_____

_____

_____

_____

_____

_____

_____

This is the ritual for the Nazirite: On the day that his term as Nazirite is completed, he shall be brought to the entrance of the Tent of Meeting.
—Numbers 6:13

The Nazirite alone in the history of Judaism pledged himself to God by limiting certain activities (no sex, wine, liquor, or the cutting of hair). For these pious individuals, their commitment was expressed generally only for a limited, self-determined period of time. Nevertheless, the Bible does record that Samson's parents had dedicated his entire life to being a Nazirite. For most of the others, their time-limited commitment was celebrated after their period of service at the Tent of Meeting (the desert Tabernacle), where the Jewish community enjoyed God's presence. Then, they returned to their normal lives in the community and became like everyone else. But were their lives ever the same? They were not. After mourning, are ours? They are not. As part of our mourning, we celebrate the life of our deceased—and then we return to the community.

PERSONAL REFLECTIONS

_____

_____

_____

_____

> . . . *thus says Adonai, God: "Behold I am about*
> *to take the people of Israel from the nations*
> *where they went; I will gather them from all*
> *around and bring them back to their soil."*
> —Ezekiel 37:21

*A*s we have seen throughout his writings, the prophet Ezekiel offers hope to the Israelites in the midst of their exile. After nearly fifty years, some of the exiles chose not to go home. They either adopted new lives in Babylonia or continued to journey to other lands. Even those who chose to go back to Israel could only do so once they understood that the land had changed. It was no longer the Israel that they had left behind. The "land" we left before we became mourners has also changed. While we cannot return to a past as it once was, we must still find a way to embrace it. The memory of the past is now part of our present as it guides us into an optimistic future.

PERSONAL REFLECTIONS

_____

_____

_____

_____

_____

A Meditation
Before Saying Kaddish

୧୬୬ୡ

There are times when each of us feels lost or alone, adrift and forsaken, unable to reach those next to us, or to be reached by them. And there are days and nights when existence seems to lack all purpose, and our lives seem brief sparks in an indifferent cosmos.

Fear and loneliness enter into the soul. None of us is immune from doubt and fear; none escapes times when all seems dark and senseless. Then, at the ebbtide of the spirit, the soul cries out and reaches for companionship.

—*GATES OF PRAYER*

Outlook

> *Now Joshua, son of Nun, was filled with the*
> *spirit of wisdom because Moses had laid his*
> *hands upon him; and the Israelites heeded him,*
> *doing as Adonai had commanded Moses.*
>
> —Deuteronomy 34:9

*C*hange in leadership is seldom easy. As mourners, our roles often change. We may become the new leaders of our families, businesses, and organizations. Moses appointed Joshua as his successor because he was "filled with the spirit of wisdom." But how did he reach this level of wisdom? It had to be more than just a transfer of authority. Perhaps it was a result of Joshua's relationship with the Divine that he had established earlier in his life. We just don't know. As you take on new roles in your family and community, remember what the deceased taught you and remember what you have learned from mourning. Then go out, like Joshua, and take the people into the Promised Land.

PERSONAL REFLECTIONS

_____

_____

_____

_____

_____

One who has a feeling of shame will not sin;
but it is certain that the ancestors of one who has
no feeling of shame did not stand at the foot of
Mount Sinai.
—Babylonian Talmud, *Nedarim* 20a

*W*hether we are rich or poor, the rituals of mourning are the same for each individual Jew. Nevertheless, each of us chooses to mourn in our individual ways. In the process, we come to understand a great deal about our relationship with the deceased. Many things may surface that previously have gone unnoticed. We have to be honest about our relationships with people who are now deceased. Some may feel that this loved one chained us to the past. Others may fear that since our loved one encouraged us to move forward, we may find it more difficult to be motivated to make progress in our lives on our own without his or her assistance. Here, the Talmud comes to teach us a difficult lesson: Let go of the past and boldly embrace the future.

PERSONAL REFLECTIONS

_____

_____

_____

_____

Tuesday/Yom Shelishi _____ (today's date)

The heavens declare the glory of God.
—Psalm 19:2

To move from the past and all it represents is a difficult task that may take more psychic energy than we seem to have. While much of our work in this regard will take place during this month of mourning, the process will continue beyond it. So how do we gain the strength necessary to do the hard work of mourning yet to be done? Some will say that we should reach deeply inside of ourselves, into the reservoir of strength that lays deep beneath the recesses of the soul. Others will take their lead from the Psalmist, who suggests that we look to the heavens for strength and fortitude, for they "declare the glory of God," the real source of our strength no matter where we find it.

PERSONAL REFLECTIONS

_____

_____

_____

_____

_____

_____

As droplets that come down upon herbs refresh them and make them beautiful, so words of Torah refresh those who study them and make them beautiful.

—Sifre to Deuteronomy 30:6

Such simple truths as the one above are often found in the most obvious places: "Torah is life." In the process of study, we enrich the text and add to its historical development. We may even deceive ourselves into believing that we have added meaning to it. But the purpose of the process is that, even as we reflect upon Torah, it restores us. This process has nurtured our people throughout our history. But we have to work at it, since renewal does not just come of its own volition. So continue your study. As the rabbis of *Pirke Avot*, a rabbinic volume of practical wisdom, have suggested, "Make study a fixed habit."

PERSONAL REFLECTIONS

_____

_____

_____

_____

_____

_____

Strength and joy are in God's place.
—1 Chronicles 16:27

*M*ourning may weaken the spirit. At the same time, the process of mourning that is prescribed by our tradition strengthens us. Although regaining our strength is a major accomplishment, it is not enough to accomplish during the mourning period. We also have to recapture our sense of joy. It may sound trite, but we have to learn to laugh again, especially in the midst of our pain. We can find both strength and joy in the presence of God. But how do we ascertain God's presence? Where do we find God? The students of the enigmatic Rabbi of Kotzk asked their teacher the same question. His reply, "Wherever you let God into your lives."

PERSONAL REFLECTIONS

_____

_____

_____

_____

_____

_____

> *At the end of forty days, Noah opened the*
> *window of the ark that he had made.*
>
> —Genesis 8:6

*A*ccording to Genesis, it rained forty days and forty nights during the time of Noah as God attempted to wash the earth clean. After the rains, Noah sent out a raven, but that bird did not return. After waiting a while, Noah sent out a dove, which returned with an olive branch in her beak. This told him that dry land had begun to reappear. God then cast a rainbow in the sky, representing the Divine promise to Noah and to all humankind. This indicated that the rains were finally over. Noah would not look back at the past and its destruction. Once the ark came to rest, Noah, with God's help, began the process of rebuilding. You can do the same.

PERSONAL REFLECTIONS

_____

_____

_____

_____

_____

_____

> *Now Solomon sat on the throne of his father*
> *David, and his rule was secure and strong.*
> —1 Kings 2:12

*S*olomon succeeded David on the throne. While we know from the Scriptures that David was not without moral imperfection, that he was flawed like all of us, David was a remarkable leader. As might be expected, it was difficult for Solomon to succeed his father. However, Solomon led the Jewish people with the kind of insightful wisdom that makes for legends. He was given the privilege of building the Temple in Jerusalem. Solomon made a name for himself that evolved independently of his father. We can all do the same. While we stand on the shoulders of those whom we mourn, we can reach higher as a result of the foundation they provided for us. So stand tall and reach beyond the past.

PERSONAL REFLECTIONS

_____

_____

_____

_____

_____

_____

A Meditation
Before Saying Kaddish

⟨∞⟩

That cry of the heart is where prayer begins. We reach out in anger or need for something which we feel is beyond our power. While prayer can amplify our feelings, it can also calm or soothe them. . . . We can assume, then, that prayer's soothing effect is one of the reasons people pray. This can be true whether or not one believes or, even, understands the words of the prayers. In fact, Kaddish is not chanted in Hebrew, but in Aramaic, the language spoken in the land of Israel when rabbinic Judaism was first evolving.

There may be certain advantages to saying a prayer in a language which is not familiar to you. When you don't know what the words really mean, they may resonate in a deeper, more primitive way than if the words had meaning. They may affect you on preverbal and sensory levels. You may be so moved by their sound, tune, and rhythm that you rock or sway to them as you intone them. This motion, which is often seen among Jews in deep prayer, has been the cadence for one generation after another around the globe. The power of that connection is greater than words.

—ANNE BRENER, *MOURNING & MITZVAH*

NINE

Coming to Accept

*Teach us, therefore, to number our days
so that we may attain a heart of wisdom.*
—Psalm 90:12

The months of the mourning period are designed to provide us with the opportunity to study the texts of our tradition and to fully examine our lives in the context of our relationship with others. In doing so, we are helped by the words of our tradition to accept the death of the one we love. At the same time, the words of our prophets, particularly when they are accompanied by the later insights of our sages, afford us a renewed sense of hope for our lives as they direct all of us toward a messianic future of redemption. As we move through our lives, we come to understand—as did our ancestors—that Jewish history is not just a series of events recorded over time. Instead, Jewish history—which is identified by its perpetual pattern of hope—has direction and purpose. While it records the encounters of the Jewish people with God throughout time, it also chronicles events that can bring us to a more "perfect time," to *mashiach-zeit*, the time of the Messiah.

But when is this messianic time and how do we help it arrive? The rabbis of the Babylonian Talmud (*Sanhedrin*

98a) teach us that the messianic period will arrive "today—*if you would hearken to God's voice*" (Psalm 95:7). When we listen carefully, we can hear God's voice in the words of our tradition. That's the main reason we make sacred study part of our daily routine: to receive God's guidance, teaching us how and why to accept Divine guidance and have hope. So during this month, as we have come to accept the death of the one we loved, we continue our study. And as we do, we keep in mind the words of Hannah Senesh, the daring young freedom fighter from Budapest who perished during World War II. They help heal the heart and help us to learn to accept: "There are stars whose light reaches the earth only after they themselves have disintegrated and are no more. And there are people whose scintillating memory lights the world after they have passed from it. These lights which shine in the darkest night are those which illumine for us the path."

Recognition

> For *he saw that the resting place was good and*
> *that the land was pleasant. He bowed his*
> *shoulder to bear and became a servant under task work.*
> —Genesis 49:15

*N*ear the end of Jacob's life, he called his sons together and blessed them. Contained in each blessing was a prophecy, a divinely inspired prediction for what the future held for each brother. Each would receive a portion of the land. This verse from Genesis contains most of Issachar's blessing. In receiving his father's blessing, he accepted both the impending death of his father and the legacy that he left him. Then he tried to live his life in accord with the spiritual legacy that was bequeathed to him. He knew that he would have to work for it and, at times, bear a significant burden. So "he bowed his shoulder" and got ready to confront whatever was thrown his way.

PERSONAL REFLECTIONS

_____

_____

_____

_____

_____

_____

Monday/Yom Sheni _____ (today's date)

> *Death finally terminates the combat, and grief*
> *and joy, success and failures are all ended.*
> —*Union Prayer Book*

*I*t takes time to learn to accept the death of the one we loved, but we have to eventually do so. We have no other choice. For some, these nine months of mourning are an insufficient amount of time to accept the fact that our loved one is deceased. Others are able to move through the process of mourning according to the routine set by the rabbis. But no one expects you to accept the death of your loved one fully or quickly, only to begin to recognize its stark truth. However, we do gain some measure of comfort from the knowledge that death also puts an end to the daily struggle for the deceased: No more daily toil or conflict. No more racing to the finish line ahead of the next person. Only the fullness of eternal peace.

PERSONAL REFLECTIONS

_____

_____

_____

_____

_____

_____

What human shall live and not see death?
—Psalm 89:49

The Psalmist asks this question of all of us, but she is really reflecting aloud on her own pain. She is both poet and philosopher, echoing the depth of personal trauma and asking the existential question for all humankind. The more the Psalmist repeats the phrase, the more she comes to accept the reality of death. Like the Psalmist, we reflect on the same notion, recognizing the comforting power of the Psalmist's words. Indeed, who among us *can* live and not experience the death of those we love? But we do not despair. Instead, recognizing this truth offers us hope and inspiration. We realize that we do not walk the path of mourning alone and that, at one time or another, everyone else joins us.

PERSONAL REFLECTIONS

_____

_____

_____

_____

_____

_____

Wednesday/Yom Revii _____ (today's date)

I am going the way of all the earth.

—Joshua 23:14

$\mathcal{S}$ome of us were able to spend time with those we now mourn immediately prior to their death. We may only now be ready to begin to reflect on this time. Repeating the words we may have shared in the last moments of life with our deceased may offer us comfort. We go over and over them in our minds, trying to bring this memory back to life. Often, the deceased recognized when death was near. Some even spoke to us of being beckoned by what they described as an "angel of death," what my *bubbe* (grandmother) used to call the *moloch hamaves*. With these words, they accepted their impending death. In sharing their words of acceptance with us, they encouraged us to do the same.

PERSONAL REFLECTIONS

_____

_____

_____

_____

_____

_____

*Death is an illusion; its ritual uncleanness is the
symbol of its falsehood. What people call death
is the intensification and reinvigoration of life.*
— Rabbi Abraham Isaac Kook, *Orot Hakodesh*

*R*abbi Kook, the first chief rabbi of Israel, used death
to teach us about the fullness of life. Many see death as
the absolute end of life. For them, there is no existence
beyond the grave, and death is a dismal end to the challenges of daily living. But, whether death is the *end* of life
or another "stage" in it, we do not necessarily have to accept it. Acceptance does not hinge on what death is; just
our attitude toward it. The mystical Rabbi Kook did not
see death as the dark side of life nor its end. Jewish law
suggests that those who come into contact with the dead
become ritually impure. This is a guise, said Rabbi Kook.
Rather, through his own firm belief that "death" is another stage of life, Rabbi Kook encouraged us to accept
his notion that life is actually intensified through death
and that only death can bring us to immortal life.

PERSONAL REFLECTIONS

_____

_____

_____

_____

Remember and do all my mitzvot.
—Numbers 15:40

*A*t God's direction, Moses spoke these words to the people of Israel during their desert journey. It was as if to say, "As you travel far from Egyptian slavery and from the events of the past, you may be tempted to forget all that I have taught you *and* all that you have learned." Moses explained the purpose of this in the next part of this verse: "So that you can be holy unto Adonai your God." Joining memory with doing mitzvot helps ensure our holiness. As we accept our present situation, we are tempted to let go of the past entirely. It feels somehow less painful that way. But the Torah wants to remind us that there is much for us to remember.

PERSONAL REFLECTIONS

_____

_____

_____

_____

_____

_____

_____

Saturday/Shabbat   _____ (today's date)

On that day a great shofar will be sounded:
Those lost in Assyria, those banished to Egypt,
shall come back and worship Adonai
on the holy mountain, in Jerusalem.

—Isaiah 27:13

*A*t the end of our exile from Israel, proclaims the prophet, everyone will be brought back to Jerusalem. This, the center of our Jewish spiritual world, is where we will all come together and pray as a community. Yet, Isaiah's prophecy transcends time and location. The great shofar harkens future times, as well. Isaiah also speaks about our personal exile that will be brought to an end. And finally, the prophet hints at the end of days when we will all be brought together. His words bring us hope and comfort. As we accept the finality of life in this world, he reveals to us the possibility of a continuing life beyond this body's existence.

PERSONAL REFLECTIONS

_____

_____

_____

_____

_____

A Meditation
Before Saying Kaddish

〇〰〰〇

The melody that the loved one played upon the piano of our life will never be played quite that way again, but we must not close the keyboard and allow the instrument to gather dust. We must seek out other artists of the spirit, new friends who gradually will help us to find the road to life again, who will walk on that road with us. The establishment of new patterns of interaction with other people, beginning with the interaction of language and moving on to new avenues of creative expression is [a] law for the conquest of grief and the conquest of death.

—JOSHUA LOTH LIEBMAN

Acknowledgment

Sunday/Yom Rishon _____ (today's date)

> *The whole earth was of one language*
> *and of one speech.*
>
> —Genesis 11:1

*A*ccording to the Torah, everyone spoke the same language before the episode at the Tower of Babel. It seems like this universal language would have made for clearer communication between people. But as the story is related in the Torah, the tower project became more important than anything else, and people lost sight of what they were really trying to accomplish: getting closer to God. Sometimes it is difficult to understand the feelings of one another even when we speak the same language. Often, this results from people expressing their feelings in ways that appear odd to us. We may find that as we are trying to find the right words to express how we feel at this point in our mourning, others may be doing the same.

PERSONAL REFLECTIONS

_____

_____

_____

_____

_____

_____

/Monday/Yom Sheni _____ (today's date)

> *Death is the means of transformation to a*
> *future life which is the ultimate goal of*
> *mortal existence.*
> —Saadia Gaon, *Emunot Vedeot*

*S*aadia Gaon, a tenth-century philosopher/theologian who led the Sura Academy in Baghdad, reflects the traditional Jewish wisdom that this life is merely a portal to the world-to-come. As a result, we spend our entire lives preparing for the moment of death. It is one of the reasons why the rabbis suggest that we repent on the day before our death, in addition to the other times throughout the year, such as on Yom Kippur. While the rabbis—who were the ones to introduce the Jewish community to the notion of eternal life in the next world—seldom offer the details about this future life, they do provide us with selected insights. Thus, death is not the end to life. Instead, it is merely a description of a transitional state that occurs as we prepare to move from this world to the next.

PERSONAL REFLECTIONS

_____

_____

_____

_____

_____

> *One event happens to them all.*
> —Ecclesiastes 2:14

*E*cclesiastes observed life as he experienced it. He did so to share his insights with others. While people still have to experience things on their own before they can accept certain truths, Ecclesiastes tried to teach others about the mistakes that he had made, hoping that he could prevent them from the same errors. This was not always possible. Through the experiences of his life, he developed a faith in God that I have come to appreciate perhaps more than any other biblical figure. Ecclesiastes reflected a frank understanding of all aspects of reality, whether they are filled with darkness or light. One of his observations surpassed all the rest he made: No matter how rich or poor we may be, we must accept death as an inevitable feature of life. That gives us comfort. We may not all live the same, but we all die the same.

PERSONAL REFLECTIONS

_____

_____

_____

_____

_____

No day without night and no night without day.
—*Zohar* I, 162a

While reflecting on the creation of the world, the *Zohar* offers us a prism for understanding life. We cannot fully appreciate the light of day without comparing it to the darkness of night. We may curse the darkness—or we can light candles to dispel its gloom. Whatever we do, we recognize that it is light that repels the darkness. Even so, the light may cast a shadow. We experience much of life through such puzzling polarities. Similarly, death is life's twin. It is not evil. Just as darkness is the absence of light, death is merely the absence of life. Rabbi Jonathan Omer-Man offers us this insight: The light is far away. The only way to see it is to close your eyes.

PERSONAL REFLECTIONS

_____

_____

_____

_____

_____

_____

> *Souls residing in Gan Eden are very powerful.*
> *Because of their prayers, the earthly world*
> *continues to exist.*
>
> —Anne Brener, *Mourning & Mitzvah*

*A*s mourners, we direct our prayers toward God. In such prayers as the traditional *El Maleh Rachamim*, we ask God to give our deceased eternal rest. In so doing, we fully acknowledge the death of the one we love. It has taken time to do this and it certainly has not been easy, but we are finally prepared to accept it. We believe that our prayers can move the hand of God, so to speak. Throughout this mourning process, we are preoccupied with the life of the deceased after death. But we seldom think about what our deceased do for us. Anne Brener teaches us important Torah: We may pray for the deceased, but it is their prayers that provide us with life.

PERSONAL REFLECTIONS

_____

_____

_____

_____

_____

_____

> *One law for the native and the*
> *stranger among you.*
>
> —Exodus 12:49

*T*hroughout the mourning process, we have learned that death is not reserved for only a select few among us. It is the way that we must all travel on this earth. Regardless of our individual walks of life, we are all destined to become mourners, some sooner, some later. This recognition may bring us closer to those around us. Others may seek us out, and we have to find a way to welcome them with open arms. As we attend a local synagogue so that we may say Kaddish with a minyan, we may meet people whose circumstances are dissimilar to our own. However, their mourning—and our own—has the potential to bring us closer together. From strangers we can become friends.

PERSONAL REFLECTIONS

_____

_____

_____

_____

_____

_____

_____

I shall go to him, but he will not return to me.
—2 Samuel 12:23

*C*ertainly the death of a child is the most difficult pain that any parent is forced to bear. Although David was a powerful king, he was not spared the death of his unnamed infant son, who was born to him and to Batsheva. Joining every other mourner, he had to mourn in the same way that we all do. According to the Bible, David wondered to himself, "Now that he is dead, should I fast? Can I bring him back again?" (2 Samuel 12:23). At the end of his mourning, King David verbalized the acceptance of his son's death. In the pain of his bereavement, he rose and returned to serve his people. Surely, we can follow his example and do the same.

PERSONAL REFLECTIONS

_____

_____

_____

_____

_____

_____

A Meditation
Before Saying Kaddish

⟨⟨⟨⟩⟩⟩

It is a bittersweet truth, this breathing out and breathing in. But we acknowledge and understand it. Even as we stake our lives and the lives of our children on it. Like fallen leaves enriching the soil, it is true. This return of the genes and the generations must occur if new ones are to set out.

—RABBI LAWRENCE KUSHNER, *THE RIVER OF LIGHT*

Affirmation

Sunday/Yom Rishon _____ (today's date)

> *Would that all of God's people*
> *would be prophets!*
> —Numbers 11:29b

Prophets are messengers of God who speak on God's behalf. They are also able to foretell the future. According to the Bible, some prophets like Jonah were reluctant to respond to God's call. Even Moses was initially diffident, afraid that he was unworthy of the task. All prophets have a special relationship with God. As a result, they know things will take place even before they happen. Sometimes we wonder whether things would have been different had we known about the death of a loved one before death occurred. We may have thought about that a great deal over the past nine months. Even when death is imminent, we never know when a person will die. Surely, we are not prophets. We can only accept life as it is.

PERSONAL REFLECTIONS

Monday/Yom Sheni _____ (today's date)

> *Death is the absence of life . . .*
> *there is no evil in it.*
> —Morris Raphael Cohen

$\mathcal{W}$e generally tend to think of death as inherently evil because it is the end of life as we know it. Indeed, death and the mourning that accompanies it completely changes our lives. Death tears the one we love from us. It is heart-wrenching and painful, but it is not evil, since life itself is always evolving and changing. We have finally learned during these nine months of mourning that death is merely the absence of present life and that it is not the end of all life. As Rabbi Maurice Lamm taught, "The spirit is mightier than the grave." And the life of the spirit transcends all space and time.

PERSONAL REFLECTIONS

_____

_____

_____

_____

_____

_____

_____

Life, not death, is the human's misfortune.
—Eleazar ben Yair, in Josephus, *Jewish War* 7.8.7

*E*leazar ben Yair, the leader of the Jewish community at Masada, confronted his own death and the end of his entire community. After fighting the Roman soldiers for many months, death was a conscious act for them that defied victory to the Romans, who would have enslaved or killed the Jews. In this final speech to the community at Masada, Eleazar said that death "gives liberty to the soul and permits it to depart to its own pure abode, there to be free from all calamity." Death frees the soul and the spirit, so we must not be bound to it. We have to find the strength to mourn, to accept death, and then to continue living. It is the only courageous choice we have.

PERSONAL REFLECTIONS

_____

_____

_____

_____

_____

_____

> *This is not . . . about death. If anything, it is . . .*
> *about life. It is not about how we live,*
> *but about the meaning of life.*
> —Rabbi Neil Gillman, *The Death of Death*

*I*t may seem like our primary focus these past nine months has been on the one who has died. However, mourning and bereavement are not about death. The entire process of mourning is really about life. During this period of mourning, we have come to finally and fully accept the stark reality of death, but we have learned much about how we now need to live, the changes we have to make in our lives. For example, the time we spend with those we love now takes on a new significance. We have probably already made many of these changes, but there will be more in the months ahead. Through these changes, we will also honor the memory of our deceased and perpetuate the values they taught us.

PERSONAL REFLECTIONS

_____

_____

_____

_____

_____

*No one can claim to be wise about life whose
wisdom does not include a relationship to death.*
—Rabbi Jack Riemer

*W*e must all confront the reality of death. We cannot avoid it. By this point in our mourning, we have finally realized this painful truth. Nevertheless, we may try to shield others from it, particularly very young children. Perhaps we think that since they will have to eventually face death, why make them do so now? We may also think that by shielding others we are somehow protecting ourselves as well. However, confronting the past through mourning may help them gain wisdom that will help them face other challenges in life. The wisdom may be difficult for them to learn but will bolster them in the years ahead. According to Rabbi Riemer, a confrontation with death provides all of us with the most profound way to gain wisdom.

PERSONAL REFLECTIONS

_____

_____

_____

_____

_____

And Abraham and Sarah became old.
—Genesis 18:11

The Bible records the aging of Abraham and Sarah as an overnight occurrence, but we know that we do not suddenly grow old. Growing takes place over a lifetime. Perhaps this statement from Genesis is a way for the Bible to foreshadow the impending death of Abraham and Sarah. Or perhaps it is a way to indicate the profundity of their wisdom, the result of a full and rich life. It may run counter to our intuition, but older adults generally do not fear death. They may fear dependence, but they are not afraid to face their own mortality. It is younger people who fear death, perhaps because older people have experienced life and grown in their wisdom as a result of it.

PERSONAL REFLECTIONS

> *Nations will walk by your light and sovereign*
> *rulers by your shining radiance.*
>
> —Isaiah 60:3

*A*t first, we might think that the prophet Isaiah is speaking about God, but it seems that he is really speaking about Jerusalem. Anyone who has been to Jerusalem knows how the city captures light, so much so that it is called "Jerusalem of gold." But the light it radiates is a light that is captured from the days to come, the messianic era, according to Isaiah. But then Isaiah goes on to trace the source of Jerusalem's light, and we find in these days of mourning that it is the source of our light as well: "The sun shall no longer be your light by day . . . but Adonai will be to you an everlasting light" (Isaiah 60:19).

PERSONAL REFLECTIONS

_____

_____

_____

_____

_____

_____

_____

A Meditation Before Saying Kaddish

꘎꘎꘎

I am standing upon a seashore. A ship at my side spreads her white sails to the morning breeze and starts for the blue ocean. She is an object of beauty and strength, and I stand and watch her until at length she is only a ribbon of white cloud just where the sea and sky come to mingle with each other.

Then someone at my side says, "There, she's gone!" Gone where? Gone from my sight—that is all. She is just as large in mast and hull and spar as she was when she left my side, and just as able to bear her load of living freight to the place of destination. Her diminished size is in me, not in her!

And just at the moment when someone at my side says, "There, she's gone!" there are other voices ready to take up the glad shout, "Here, she comes!" And that is dying!

—Colonel David (Mickey) Marcus

Determination

Sunday/Yom Rishon _____ (today's date)

> *Adonai . . . cast them into another land*
> *as the day.*
> —Deuteronomy 29:27

*T*his verse from Deuteronomy speaks about the future dispersion of the Israelites from Jerusalem. And even though they returned, it was never the same as it had been before they were cast out of the land. According to the sage Rabbi Akiva, it means that the day comes and goes and never returns. But Rabbi Eliezer said that the text means that as the day starts with darkness and then lights up, so the darkness of those in exile is destined to be lighted up again (Babylonian Talmud, *Sanhedrin* 110b). For us, we have learned as we mourn that we may feel that the past is behind us and will never return, but the life we enjoyed with the deceased represents a light that will forever illumine our future path.

PERSONAL REFLECTIONS

_____

_____

_____

_____

_____

_____

In each incarnation, we weave or unravel a few more stitches in the garment of light. At a certain point, one has finished and can go home.

—Rabbi Jonathan Omer-Man

Rabbi Omer-Man's teaching reflects a mystical notion in Judaism that offers us insight and some measure of comfort as we reflect on the past and prepare for the remainder of our own lives, something that the mourning process has helped us to do. According to this idea, people do re-enter life in some form; they are reincarnated in succeeding generations. With each incarnation, they improve their souls through the work of *teshuvah*, repentance, until they have finished their work and can return home to God. I don't know whether souls are reincarnated, but I certainly believe that there are things that I don't fully understand or can't explain, what I like to call "windows on the world." And so I like to keep these windows open.

PERSONAL REFLECTIONS

_____

_____

_____

_____

_____

Tuesday/Yom Shelishi _____ (today's date)

At death, he has already entered the harbor—
the haven of rest in the world-to-come.
                                    —*Exodus Rabbah* 48:1

*S*ome Jewish writers imagine death as a ship that enters the harbor after a journey at sea. For some, the ocean voyage may be long. For others, it is unfortunately a short and difficult trip on a storm-tossed sea. Nevertheless, it is somewhat ironic that we usually join together to celebrate whenever a ship begins its voyage. We eagerly anticipate the exciting travel that lies ahead. So why indeed should we cheer on the ship's return, particularly if we understand that it implies death? Here the rabbis of the midrash offer us insight: As we mourn, we think about the life journey of the deceased. Now that our loved one has entered the harbor, he or she is at rest, awaiting the next voyage to the world-to-come.

PERSONAL REFLECTIONS

_____

_____

_____

_____

_____

Wednesday/Yom Revii _____ (today's date)

Prayer is about the tension we feel at the imperfection of the universe . . . about exile and alienation and about letting God back in.
—Rabbi Abraham Joshua Heschel

*S*ome of us may not have done much real praying prior to our recent encounter with death. As we look back upon these nine months of mourning, we may find that prayers have filled our hearts and our days during the entire period. At times, the prayers brimmed with anger. At other times, they were filled with bitterness. But they were always offerings of the heart. We finally understand that prayer is not about asking and receiving. Instead, it is about an evolving dialogue with the Divine. Like mourning, prayer is a process. It starts with what we feel about the world, how we feel about losing the one we love through death, and then finally—after months of searching—of letting God back into our lives.

PERSONAL REFLECTIONS

_____

_____

_____

_____

_____

Thursday/Yom Chamishi _____ (today's date)

> *You are eternally mighty, Adonai. You revive the dead [give life to all], great is your power to save.*
>
> —*Amidah*

This line begins the second paragraph of the *Amidah*, the set of benedictions that forms the core of every worship service. Often, we rush through the words without giving much thought to their meaning. Some prayer books have changed the words to read "give life to all" instead of "revive the dead," but the sentiment is the same. This theological notion may make some people uncomfortable while bringing comfort to others: At the end of days, however and whenever that will come, God will bring all of our souls together for eternal life. And then we will be able to join the deceased once again. Here, in the midst of prayer, the past and the future become merged through the power of the Almighty. Thank God.

PERSONAL REFLECTIONS

_____

_____

_____

_____

_____

_____

Friday/Yom Shishi _____ (today's date)

> *So God banished him from the borders*
> *[of the Garden].*
>
> —Genesis 3:23

*A*fter Adam ate from the forbidden tree, he and Eve were prohibited from returning to the Garden. According to Genesis, flaming swords prevented them from re-entering Paradise once they were expelled. God wanted to make sure that there was no misunderstanding. They had to separate from the past and remake their lives out in the world. An initial read of the text suggests that they would have been better off in Eden. But with knowledge came a frank confrontation with reality, with life and death. No, once we have left the past, just as Adam and Eve were forced out of the Garden, we cannot return to it. Mourning has taught us that. But we can rebuild our lives anew. We have learned that, as well.

PERSONAL REFLECTIONS

_____

_____

_____

_____

_____

_____

Saturday/Shabbat _____ (today's date)

God will destroy death forever. My God will
wipe the tears away from all faces.
—Isaiah 25:8

*J*t seems too hard to believe that God will rid the world of death. This is Isaiah's messianic vision for the future. At the end of time as we know it, no longer will we feel the pain of the survivor, what we feel each day during our mourning. But why mention this idea on Shabbat? Because Shabbat offers us a foretaste of that world. According to author, poet, and playwright Deena Metzger, "Sabbath exists in the midst of devastation. . . . This is the Sabbath: A little rain in the midst of drought, vision in the very moment of understanding nothing, a flash of beauty in a broken bowl and the miraculous insistent vitality of the body and the heart."

PERSONAL REFLECTIONS

_____

_____

_____

_____

_____

_____

A Meditation
Before Saying Kaddish

To the living—
Death is a wound. Its name is grief.
        Its companion is loneliness.
Whenever it comes—whatever its guise,
Even when there are no tears—
Death is a wound.

But death belongs to life—
        As night belongs to day
        As darkness belongs to light
        As shadows belongs to substance—
As the fallen leaf to the tree,
        As time to eternity,
        So death belongs to life.

It is not our purpose to live forever.
        It is only our purpose to live.
It is no added merit that life is long.
        It is of merit only that we make life good.

—RABBI ALVIN I. FINE

TEN

The Path
Toward Healing

God has given.
God has taken away.
Praised is the name of God.
—Job 1:21

We achieve wisdom as we learn to accept the variety of life's rich experiences. Our sacred literature gives us a prism through which to view these life experiences. As we study the texts of Jewish tradition, particularly what the prophets had to say, we gain insight and perspective. These prophets learned much about life by living it. But wisdom comes from a variety of places. The rabbis in *Pirke Avot*, a book of aphorisms penned by numerous sages, claim that the wise person learns from all people and from all situations. Thus, wisdom does not automatically result from simply accruing more years or more experiences. Wisdom is much more. Sometimes we gain bits of wisdom at times and places when we least expect it, always aware that God is our teacher.

If we trace the development of Joseph's life, we can find a model for wisdom in the Bible. Joseph's life in the Bible took many unexpected turns. He moved from being a brother to being a servant to being an acclaimed leader in Egypt. Toward the end of the Joseph story, he is reunited with his brothers. As we read the text, we can feel the embrace of these brothers who had been separated for so many years. Joseph came to understand and accept God's role in his life when he told his brothers not to berate themselves for having sold him into slavery. He says, "God sent me here, not you" (Genesis 45:8). In doing so, he teaches us that God plays a primary role in each of our lives. Job, while a much more tragic figure than Joseph, also came to understand and accept his life when he reached deeply inside of himself and found the strength to declare, "God has given. God has taken away. Praised is the name of God" (Job 1:21).

The prophets teach us a great deal about acceptance. While they teach us not to accept things the way they are—in fact, they often *demand* that we change things when we see them as morally corrupt—they do teach us to accept the role that God plays in our lives and in the day-to-day workings of the world, whether the outcome is tragic or triumphant. It is through recognizing God's presence in our lives and in the world that we can gain healing of the spirit and the soul.

Wholeness

Sunday/Yom Rishon _____ (today's date)

Adonai, absolve Your people Israel
whom You redeemed.

—Deuteronomy 21:8a

*A*s we move into the final stages of mourning, thoughts of remorse still remain with us. We may not be able to determine the origin of these thoughts or even clearly define them. So we turn to God for help, for healing, and for strength. However, healing is never fully complete. It is a process that helps shape our lives. So we pray that God may give us the courage to move forward with our lives, absolved of any guilt that we may yet feel, and bring this healing to others. Once we feel that this burden has been lifted from us, we may indeed rebuild our lives—in the fullness of our relationship with God that reflects the covenant at Sinai.

PERSONAL REFLECTIONS

_____

_____

_____

_____

_____

_____

_____

Monday/Yom Sheni _____ (today's date)

> *Weeping may linger in the evening,*
> *but joy comes in the morning.*
>
> —Psalm 30:6

*F*or many, the entire process of mourning feels like one long, solitary night. The Psalmist understands this notion and shares the profound nature of our pain. In simple verse, she speaks to us out of the depth of her own experience. Like all of us, she understands what it is like to lose one that we love—and to rebuild personal courage and inner strength through the process of mourning. She finds healing in a world that includes life as well as death and wants us to do the same. While our evenings may still be lonely and the nights remain long, joy always comes in the morning. Like God's presence in your life, this joy is something on which you can always count.

PERSONAL REFLECTIONS

_____

_____

_____

_____

_____

_____

_____

Peace heals.
When your own world is fractured, increase your
knowledge of God. It will spawn inner peace.
When the outside world is fractured, promote the
search for truth. It will spawn universal peace.
—Rebbe Nachman of Breslov, *Likutey Moharan* 1:27,
quoted in *The Empty Chair*

*W*hat more needs to be said? The mourning process helps us achieve a sense of inner peace and calm, something that is sorely needed following the death of someone we love. That is what many of us call healing. Rebbe Nachman tells us we can reach this feeling of *shelemut* (tranquillity, inner peace, serenity) by increasing our knowledge of God by studying Torah. Then we can use our study of Torah as a prism through which to view the entire world. This is particularly helpful as we look for ways to take what we have become accustomed to during mourning, such as regular study, and prepare to make these behaviors a routine part of our lives.

PERSONAL REFLECTIONS

_____

_____

_____

_____

Rabbi Hama son of Rabbi Hanina said:
"Great is repentance for it brings healing to the
world, as it is said, "I will heal their affliction,
generously I will take them back in love"
(Hosea 14:5).
—Babylonian Talmud, *Yoma* 86a

When we are first in mourning, people are more ready than at any other time to forgive us for things that we say or do that offend. As the mourning period draws to a close, people are not as willing to forgive us. They get impatient and expect us to return to a regular routine. They have also become uncomfortable with our mourning. That makes this passage from the Talmud so important right now. We can bring repentance into our mourning. And as we do, we can bring healing to the world. And with it will come the healing that we still so sorely need.

PERSONAL REFLECTIONS

_____

_____

_____

_____

_____

_____

*Do not fear death. It is just a matter of going
from one room to another, ultimately to the most
beautiful room.*
—Rabbi Menachem Mendl of Kotzk

*D*uring the early weeks of mourning, people avoid discussing philosophy and theology with us. Instead, they try only to offer us words of comfort. But after months of mourning, we now want to confront some of the issues that have been on our mind. These months have given us plenty of opportunity to reflect on the relationship between death and life. The Kotzker Rebbe reminds us not to fear death even as we contemplate it, since death is merely a stage in life that leads us to eternal life itself. Ben Sira, a Jerusalem sage who lived in the second century B.C.E. and was the author of the work known as the *Wisdom of Ben Sira*, said it another way: "Do not fear death. It is your destiny" (Ben Sira 41:3).

PERSONAL REFLECTIONS

_____

_____

_____

_____

_____

_____

Friday/Yom Shishi _____ (today's date)

Heal her, O God, please heal her.
—Numbers 12:13

These words from the Book of Numbers were uttered by Moses when his sister Miriam was stricken with leprosy. They have become somewhat of a credo for the present Jewish healing movement in North America. It is the shortest prayer in the Torah and the first that addresses healing. For many people, including me, this verse of only five Hebrew words has become a personal *kavannah* (Jewish mantra-like text) for healing. In it is contained all that I feel in a gentle but demanding plea to God. Usually, we think of prayers of healing for those who are physically ill. But as we mourn, we recognize that these words are directed to us, as well. For we all need to be healed. And so we pray, "Heal us, O God, please heal us."

PERSONAL REFLECTIONS

_____

_____

_____

_____

_____

_____

You who are afflicted, tempest-tossed,
unable to be comforted,
Behold I will set your stones with fair colors,
And lay your foundations with sapphires. . . .
All of your children will be taught of Adonai;
And great will be the peace of your children
—Isaiah 54:11, 13

*W*henever our people experienced the pain that accompanies personal exile, the Hebrew prophets offered them a *nechemta*, a message of comfort. That's why the writings of the prophets are brimming with hope and inspiration. We should review their words regularly. This idea permeated much of Jewish culture so that we are instructed to always end our messages to others—even words of rebuke—with words of consolation. In this powerful image that the rabbis have placed in the Torah reading cycle next to the story of Noah and the Flood, Isaiah's poetry speaks directly to us. Whenever we feel discomfort, even after ten months of mourning, God will bring us peace. Moreover, God will bring tranquillity and security to our children. What more could we ask for?

PERSONAL REFLECTIONS

_____

_____

_____

A Meditation
Before Saying Kaddish

⎯⎯⎯⎯⎯ ◇◊◇ ⎯⎯⎯⎯⎯

*G*od really does create the world anew daily. This is one of the things it is hard to believe when we are in mourning. It is hard to believe that anything new will ever happen that could transform the way we presently feel. And, rationally, it doesn't make sense. After all, another love doesn't replace the lost love. What makes creation new is not that there are other loves but that *we* can become other. That is where the healing comes in. If we didn't change, the fact that there were others to love would be irrelevant; we wouldn't be open to them. We discover that there are others to love *because* we are healed—not as a means of healing. So it is God who brings about healing. God enters into the emptiness of our loss. God accepts our rage, our confusion, our pain. And slowly, gradually, organically, God shapes us to grow in a new way.

—CAROL OCHS

Wholeness

Sunday/Yom Rishon _____ (today's date)

God heard the prayer of the lad . . .
—Genesis 21:17

*W*ithout fully thinking through the consequences, Sarah forced Abraham to cast out Hagar and her son Ishmael. She was jealous and frightened of them. It was a difficult time in the lives of our ancestors, an episode of which many of us are not proud. And so Ishmael prayed to God out of his pain. God heard the boy's plea to be reunited with his father. Often, in the midst of our pain, we do things without thinking. We lash out at others so we can protect ourselves. This is particularly true during the early days of mourning. Now months later we have the chance to repair the mistakes we may have made. With such repairs, we can all be brought back to wholeness.

PERSONAL REFLECTIONS

_____

_____

_____

_____

_____

_____

*I believe with complete faith that the human soul
was beautiful when it was breathed into the
individual by God and is therefore eternal.*

—Moses Maimonides

*T*he great medieval philosopher, Moses Maimonides, also known as the Rambam, taught that there are "thirteen principles of faith" that compose the foundation of Jewish religion. Many of us wrestle with these principles all the time. It is normal—even expected—that we do. To struggle with one's beliefs is part of having "complete faith" in Judaism. We come to understand this particular principle during mourning. It is part of the healing process that we are now experiencing. We know that the soul of our beloved deceased was beautiful when he or she was alive. And now that our beloved is no longer alive, the soul remains eternal. With this knowledge, we affirm that they are at peace, as are we.

PERSONAL REFLECTIONS

_____

_____

_____

_____

_____

Tuesday/Yom Shelishi　　＿＿＿＿＿＿　(today's date)

> *And the mystery we call life . . . human beings*
> *created in God's image, share in God's eternality*
> *despite the mystery we call death.*
> —Rabbi Eugene B. Borowitz

As each day has passed during our mourning, we have become increasingly comfortable with considering theological questions. These issues probably surfaced early during mourning, but we may have dismissed them in our pain. But now it is time to consider them for the direction and insight they can provide. Rabbi Borowitz, the leading liberal Jewish theologian in North America, provides us above with insight into a basic question: If we are created in God's image, then why must we face death? Borowitz argues that we share in God's eternality despite death, which will always remain a mystery to us. Yet, we can never fully know God, just as we can never completely understand death. Nevertheless, our longing for communion with the Divine burns with fiery passion in our soul.

PERSONAL REFLECTIONS

＿＿＿＿＿＿＿＿＿＿＿＿＿＿＿＿＿＿＿＿＿＿＿＿＿＿＿＿＿＿

＿＿＿＿＿＿＿＿＿＿＿＿＿＿＿＿＿＿＿＿＿＿＿＿＿＿＿＿＿＿

＿＿＿＿＿＿＿＿＿＿＿＿＿＿＿＿＿＿＿＿＿＿＿＿＿＿＿＿＿＿

＿＿＿＿＿＿＿＿＿＿＿＿＿＿＿＿＿＿＿＿＿＿＿＿＿＿＿＿＿＿

＿＿＿＿＿＿＿＿＿＿＿＿＿＿＿＿＿＿＿＿＿＿＿＿＿＿＿＿＿＿

Wednesday/Yom Revii _____ (today's date)

> *God heals up the broken heart and*
> *binds up our wounds.*
>
> —Psalm 147:3

We may not yet have fully experienced the power of God's healing. It may take time, especially during the long and painful process of mourning, but we have to open ourselves to it. Take it from those of us who have experienced it: God's healing will come. But don't just wait for it. Work toward healing by developing your own relationship with God. Build on what you have established during these past months of mourning. Find the method that works best for you. Here are some suggestions: Study by yourself and with a partner. Reflect. Take long walks. Sit quietly. Pray. Rest. Meditate. Write down your thoughts. Sing. Dance. And remember to give great big hugs to the ones you love.

PERSONAL REFLECTIONS

_____

_____

_____

_____

_____

_____

*Happy are the righteous for their days are pure
and extend to the world that is coming. When
they leave this world, all their days are sewn
together . . . radiant garments . . . to wear . . .
to the world that is coming to enjoy its pleasure.*

—*Zohar* I, 224a–b

*F*or some of us in mourning, thoughts about the after-life are merely words that try to help us understand what may have happened after our loved one died. For others, they are more than just poetic words of consolation. The idea of an afterlife and a world-to-come provides us with meaning to our entire existence here on earth. Many of us have tasted the messianic on Shabbat. And Shabbat is part of this world even though it offers us a prism into the next. Yet, some people seem to be rewarded in this world, while others go unpunished for their deeds. The *Zohar*, the core mystical text in Judaism, teaches us that good deeds pave the path for us that leads us into the next world.

PERSONAL REFLECTIONS

_____

_____

_____

_____

> *God commanded the first human, saying,*
> *"Of every tree of the garden you are free to eat,*
> *but as for the tree of knowledge of good and*
> *bad, you must not eat of it for as soon as you eat*
> *of it you shall die."*
>
> —Genesis 2:16–17

*T*ricked by the serpent, Adam and Eve ate from the tree. Most of us know the details of this story. And we recall that these first humans did not die immediately. Instead they lived for many years, although they were forced from Eden and its many blessings. As a result, they became fully human. The fullness of their humanity, which they encountered only after they left the Garden, included mortality. As our progenitors, they had no choice but to eat the fruit. The shaper of this divinely inspired moral tale had to frame the story that way, for the Torah reflects our reality. Like our early ancestors, we have all eaten of the fruits of Paradise and we must all die. Knowledge does, indeed, pave the road to truth.

PERSONAL REFLECTIONS

_____

_____

_____

_____

Saturday/Shabbat _____ (today's date)

Heal me, Adonai, and I shall be healed.
—Jeremiah 17:14

Jeremiah speaks the words of prophetic truth. Like all of us, he understands the anguish of mourning and the desire to "get through it and get on with living." His words are those of petition, but he also acts as a spokesperson for God. Jeremiah teaches us that once God heals, we are, indeed, healed. And so, echoing the words of this prophet, as part of our own mourning process, we ask God: Heal us and we shall be healed. Give us insight and understanding. May we grow from these recent challenges in our lives. Grant us courage to face the morrow. And may we be strengthened by the knowledge that You support us in all that we do.

PERSONAL REFLECTIONS

_____

_____

_____

_____

_____

_____

_____

A Meditation
Before Saying Kaddish

⟨≈⟩

*I*n every person there is a private shrine of memory and love, and in that sanctuary our loved ones abide. We sense their presence, caress their spirits, and enfold them in our hearts. They talk to us; they tell tales. Thus the pain of separation is soothed by memory, the hurt sustained is healed by love; and we ourselves become purified and ennobled through our sorrow.

—RABBI JACOB K. SHANKMAN

Tranquillity

Sunday/Yom Rishon _____ (today's date)

> *So long as earth endures, seed time and harvest,*
> *cold and heat, summer and winter, day and night*
> *shall not cease.*
>
> —Genesis 8:22

The knowledge and surety of our world gives us comfort. Even at this late stage in our mourning, things may continue to be difficult for us. The pain of our loss is diminished with each passing day, but it does not abate completely. Yet, we know that we can count on the orderliness of the world. In a world where there seems to be little on which to depend, there are indeed many things about which we can be confident. The sun rises and sets each day. One season turns into another. Seeds are sown, grow to maturity, are harvested—and the cycle of life continues. At the heart of this orderliness is God—the foundation of the entire world.

PERSONAL REFLECTIONS

_____

_____

_____

_____

_____

> *Adonai will grant strength to our people. Adonai*
> *will bless our people with peace.*
>
> —Psalm 29:11

*T*his text from Psalms is familiar to many of us. Among other things, it concludes *Birkat Hamazon*, Grace After Meals, in which we express our thanksgiving to God for many things, including the food we have eaten and the land on which it is grown. It is also a statement of resolute faith, a belief in God's goodness and power— even in the face of mourning. Each day as I sing the two lines above in the same familiar way that I have so many times before, I add my own prayer for personal strength and healing. I ask that God grant strength and healing to my brothers and sisters throughout the world who confront the daily struggles of life as I do.

PERSONAL REFLECTIONS

_____

_____

_____

_____

_____

_____

_____

Wounds heal, but words do not.
—Rabbi David Kimchi

Although they may appear to be gaping wounds that will never heal, our wounds will heal more fully with each passing day of our mourning. People continue to offer us words of comfort and consolation. People will inquire about our well-being. We may feel like their interest is short and hurried, convenient and conventional. But it is not the words themselves that heal. Rather, it is the person speaking these words that brings true healing to us, for they are messengers of the Divine. God has placed these angels on earth to care for us. Through such caring people, God can bring healing to the earth. As our tradition suggests, words that come from the heart enter the heart.

PERSONAL REFLECTIONS

_____

_____

_____

_____

_____

_____

_____

Wednesday/Yom Revii _____ (today's date)

We have been taught: A person should wash his or her face, hands and feet every day for the sake of his or her Maker.
—Babylonian Talmud, *Shabbat* 50b

*W*hen we are finally able to follow this advice of the rabbis of the Talmud by reestablishing a regular pattern that includes even the most trivial aspects of our daily routine, then we know that we are on the road to complete healing. We may also find renewed pleasure in these simple activities; they provide relief for the burden of our pain in mourning. These behaviors remind us that we have an obligation to take care of our bodies because they are lent to us by God. Our bodies provide a haven for our weary souls. As we care for God's creation, we honor our Creator.

PERSONAL REFLECTIONS

_____

_____

_____

_____

_____

_____

_____

*Happy is the person who can withstand the test
given him or her, for there is no mortal whom the
Holy One does not test. God tests the rich
person to see if his or her hands will be open to
the poor; and God tests the poor person to see if
he or she will be resigned to suffering and not be
filled with resentment.*

—*Exodus Rabbah* 31:3

Regardless of our background, rich or poor, young or old, life is indeed a test. We must all confront the many challenges that we are forced to face over the course of our lives. And the death of someone we love is among the greatest tests that we must encounter. As we near the completion of the mourning process, we can reflect on how we have grown as a result of it. Are we now more independent and self-assured? Have we discovered a reservoir of inner strength of which we were previously unaware? Did talents surface that we had forgotten about? While we would have preferred to grow through means other than mourning, we must admit to ourselves that we are stronger people because of it.

PERSONAL REFLECTIONS

_____

_____

_____

I am the God who heals you.

—Exodus 15:26

 his text from Exodus comes straight from the mouth of God, so to speak, and directly from the teachings of the Torah, so there is no mistake about it: God brings us healing. It is part of our recollection of the Exodus experience of our people that we carried with us wherever we traveled in history. It is also something that we want to hear particularly now during mourning, regardless of how far along in the process we have gone. Especially as we suffer anguish and pain, we want to be sure that God will mend us. But because it is God who speaks in Exodus 15:26 of healing, the potential for such healing is contained in this promise from God made to each one of us through our ancestors. Such healing comes in the context of a relationship with God.

PERSONAL REFLECTIONS

_____

_____

_____

_____

_____

_____

Saturday/Shabbat _____ (today's date)

A teaching of truth was in your mouth,
and no wrong was found on your lips;
you walked with Me in peace and equity,
and turned away from iniquity.

—Malachi 2:6

*M*ourning is a humbling experience. It brings even the greatest among us to our knees. No matter how powerful we may be, wealth or power is meaningless in the face of death. We all face life and death and become mourners just like everyone else. And as mourners, the prophet Malachi's words speak directly to us. They are new standards for our behavior. These are among the things that we have learned during these past months of mourning: to speak the truth, to walk peacefully with God, to steer clear of sin. These behaviors contain within them great potential for healing as we live our lives, even when we arise from mourning. As we walk with God, we become at peace with the world and with ourselves.

PERSONAL REFLECTIONS

_____

_____

_____

_____

_____

A Meditation
Before Saying Kaddish

———— ⟨⟩ ————

A piece of cloth in the process of being woven. As the shuttle moves silently back and forth, thread falls from the bobbin, laying the woof upon the warp, pass after pass, skein after skein, bolt after bolt.

At times, the spool comes to an end and a new thread is woven seamlessly into the fabric. At times, the transition is not so smooth, leaving loose ends dangling for someone else to fix. But the work of the Weaver continues, the sound of the batten and the treadle of the loom does not cease.

A piece of cloth in the process of being woven. A tapestry of memory and life.

—ANDREW DAVIDS

Inspiration

Sunday/Yom Rishon   _____ (today's date)

Adonai called to Moses and spoke to him.
—Leviticus 1:1

This is the way the third book of the Torah begins: with a call from God. This phrase is an introduction to the entire Book of Leviticus, what our tradition calls the holiness code. The instructions contained in this book of the Torah provide the Israelites with the guidance necessary to become a distinctly holy community. But this will happen only when we follow God's direction for our lives. When God calls to us, we are obliged to listen. And when God provides us with guidance for our lives, whenever it comes, particularly during this period of mourning, we are certainly obligated to listen. In mourning, we need that counsel most. God calls to us now in mourning, and we must listen once again.

PERSONAL REFLECTIONS

_____

_____

_____

_____

_____

_____

> *I found a house full of candles that were unlit.*
> *I have kindled them and the house*
> *was filled with light.*
> —Dov Baer, the Maggid of Mezritch

*T*his wonderful Hasidic teacher writes about the world in which we live. But we have to be the ones to fill this "house," which is really this world, with light. And with each candle we light, we bring healing to ourselves and to our world. As you study this week, make a difference in someone else's life to make it a little more livable for them. Depending on your own financial ability, help someone to succeed in business. Or help someone with their schooling or vocational education. Perhaps you can help with tuition support, professional advice, or tutoring. With each action you take, remember to do it in the name of the one you mourn.

PERSONAL REFLECTIONS

_____

_____

_____

_____

_____

*Before Noah's birth, what was reaped was not
what was sown. . . . But after Noah was born,
the world, the earth returned to its orderly growth.*
—*Tanchuma, Bereishit*

*G*od sent the Flood waters to cleanse the entire earth of
its corruption. Everything was affected by the Flood.
Nothing was left untouched by the waters. There was
great turmoil in the world, but soon thereafter the earth
returned to its normal pattern. Likewise, nothing in our
lives remained unaffected by our mourning. And following these many months of mourning, we cannot return to
a regular pattern of living. Instead, a new pattern has to
evolve, one that is adjusted to meet our new station in
life. Whatever we do, the world continues to follow its
own order, what the rabbis call *olam kenegdo*. And we
regain our own stability in the process.

PERSONAL REFLECTIONS

_____

_____

_____

_____

_____

_____

Wednesday/Yom Revii _____ (today's date)

The beauty and grandeur in the human spirit and
the rest of nature reminds us that tikkun
[restoration] is indeed possible.
—Rabbi Nancy Flam

*I*t is nearly impossible to explain the phenomenon, but the human spirit eventually finds renewal. Sometimes it takes longer than we would like, but this indefatigable spirit allows us to carry on our work and continue to live in the face of whatever challenge is thrown our way. Ecclesiastes understood this challenge and expressed it throughout his biblical book. Although he was often pessimistic about life, he constantly spoke about this spirit of renewal, which he saw evident in his own life and in the life of others around him. Each day, our souls are renewed. Jewish tradition even suggests that our souls are reborn every day so that we awake as "new" people. In fact, we will arise from our mourning as renewed people. You can count on it.

PERSONAL REFLECTIONS

_____

_____

_____

_____

_____

*If by chance an opportunity comes to you to
better yourself do not hesitate to seize hold of it.
It is so decreed in Heaven. Cling to it until
another opportunity comes to you.*
—Rabbi Simcha Bunem

*I*t is God who heals. Throughout our mourning, we have learned the full extent of this religious truth. Each day, as we have engaged our sacred texts and our Jewish tradition, God's healing power has been affirmed. But healing often comes to us in surprising ways: the stranger on the street, someone we may have just met, the clerk at the local grocery store. So we have to be open to others, since they may all be messengers of God. Remember that our tradition teaches that the Messiah may be living among the beggars and those who are covered with wounds. So we have to go out and look for him or her.

PERSONAL REFLECTIONS

_____

_____

_____

_____

_____

_____

> *They shall not appear before Adonai*
> *empty-handed, but each with his or her own gift,*
> *according to the blessing that Adonai your God*
> *has bestowed upon you.*
> —Deuteronomy 16:16–17

*N*o matter where we go or what we do in life, we constantly stand before God. There is no hiding or escaping. Jonah tried to flee God's mission but soon understood its impossibility. And Adam learned this lesson after he tried to hide from God's rebuke in the garden. We feel this most acutely on Yom Kippur, particularly during the concluding *Neilah* service, where the ark remains open and we stand through the majority of the service. But how do we bring ourselves to thank God, especially after enduring these months of mourning, during which we may have blamed God? The answer is simple: We just bring ourselves. God does not desire our sacrifice. God desires only ourselves: yours and mine.

PERSONAL REFLECTIONS

_____

_____

_____

_____

_____

> *Morning by morning You rouse,*
> *You rouse my ears to give heed. . . .*
> *God, You open my ears. . . .*
> —Adapted from Isaiah 50:4–5

*S*habbat offers us messages of hope and healing that support us through the week. How do we hear these messages? We have to be willing to hear them. But what happens when we are not ready or willing to hear such messages? We turn to God, as did the prophet Isaiah, and ask God to open our ears so that we may hear. Reflecting on personal prayer such as Isaiah's, Rabbi Sheldon Zimmerman framed his prayer this way: "In Your oneness, I find healing. In the promise of Your love, I am soothed. In Your wholeness, I too can become whole once again."

PERSONAL REFLECTIONS

_____

_____

_____

_____

_____

_____

_____

A Meditation
Before Saying Kaddish

⟿

Behind the pulse beat of the universe is the Infinite Spirit that animates all. It is the total manuscript of which each of us is a single syllable. From that Source has come all life—your life and my life, and all the life that ever was and ever will be. The dreams we cherish are the waking thoughts and ideas that stem from its Mind. Every flower that blooms, every snowflake, rainfall and dewfall, starshine and moonglow, every nightingale's song strumming the keyboard of the dark ether, every handclasp that pledges friendship and every kiss that seals love's betrothal—everything that is and that ever will be represents eternity pouring into our hearts. Our lives are upward steps on the altar-slopes of Infinitude. We partake in the life of God, and though we are but dust while God is everlasting, God's life and our life are one even as the Eternal Over-Soul and the geometry of the human soul are one. Nothing, nothing can ever sever their oneness.

—*Adapted from* RABBI A. ALAN STEINBACH

ELEVEN

Reaching Out to Others

The memory of the righteous shall be for a blessing. *
—Proverbs 10:7

$\mathcal{W}$e have learned a great deal after so many months of mourning, even if we never wanted to learn it. Each day forced us to face another challenge, and many people reached out to help us. Many of these acts of comfort and consolation came from people we least expected. They called, they wrote, they came to visit. We learned what Ecclesiastes meant when he said that a threefold cord cannot be broken. In other words, we gain strength through joining together to face life's challenges. Our burden seemed lessened by the presence and caring of others who provided us with support when we needed it most. Many shared their own experiences of mourning with us and assured us by the example of their own lives that we would be able to "make it." They told us that we would come through the process of mourning as stronger individuals, and we knew, from their example, that we would. To be a survivor, we were told, one has to be strong. They emphasized to us the need to follow the

---

*A phrase that is traditionally said after the name of the deceased is said aloud

mourning process as prescribed by Jewish ritual. They may have also told us about their intimate encounters with God and suggested that we develop our own relationship with the Divine.

Now is the time to offer insights to others based on our own experience. We have survived, although sometimes we are not sure how. And we now want to teach others the many things we have learned. Many others as they begin their mourning need our help, and we are finally ready to reach out to them.

We recognize that there is still much work for us to do in the months ahead and that even after the formal mourning period has concluded we will feel the need for more healing. Yet we feel "healthy enough" to help others. During our mourning, we have learned one of the truths of spiritual logic: As we extend ourselves to others, we too will find uplift of spirit.

Offering Help

Sunday/Yom Rishon _____ (today's date)

> *I call heaven and earth to witness . . . that I have*
> *set before you life and death, the blessing and the*
> *curse; therefore, choose life so that you may live,*
> *you and your seed.*
>
> —Deuteronomy 30:19

We now have the opportunity to make decisions about our mourning that will affect the rest of our lives and provide guidance and direction for those around us, particularly members of our family and close friends. Although we still feel the pain of mourning, we recognize that God has indeed set before us the opportunity to make a choice in our lives. We are like the individual who is lost in the forest and happens upon another person who is equally lost. One asks the other, "Do you know the way out?" Comes the reply, "I only know that the way I have come is the wrong way. Let us find the way out together." Blessing or curse? We all make the choice every day of our lives.

PERSONAL REFLECTIONS

_____

_____

_____

_____

_____

*The hero is one who kindles a great light in the
world, who sets up blazing torches in the dark
streets for men and women to see by.
The righteous one is the one who walks through
the dark paths of the world, and is himself
or herself a light.*

—Felix Adler

$\mathcal{W}$e have walked along dark paths for many months
now, and we have occupied many dark places. At times,
we felt frightened and alone. Others tried to illumine our
paths, and we tried to follow their examples. But ultimately, we had to walk the path alone. We learned that it
is God who provides us with the Divine light that illumines the path on which we travel. Now it is time to find
a way to help light the path for others. If we are strong
enough, if we are courageous enough, we might become
that light for others. Then we can become a prism
through which God's light might be refracted for the
world.

PERSONAL REFLECTIONS

_____

_____

_____

_____

Tuesday/Yom Shelishi _____ (today's date)

> *The world is broken at points of weakness and*
> *through our acts we can be its "fixers."*
> —Rabbi Nancy Flam

Throughout these months of mourning, we experienced many of the points of brokenness in the world. As we were able, we worked to repair some of them. We left some of them broken, unable to do the necessary repair. But now, strengthened by many months of mourning, we are indeed ready to start the work of repair. And we do so by offering to help others. Make yourself aware every day this week that as you teach someone else something of what you learned, you also invite the one you mourn into your "classroom" with you. As you savor his or her memory, that person teaches you alongside a "student" of your own.

PERSONAL REFLECTIONS

_____

_____

_____

_____

_____

_____

Rabbi Yose would say,
"Let your friend's property be as dear to you as
your own. Since you cannot inherit the Torah,
you must prepare yourself to study it.
Let all you do be for the sake of Heaven."
—*Pirke Avot* 2:12

*T*hese three principles of Rabbi Yose are important to remember during this period of mourning. First, by cherishing our friend's property, you are reminded of the value of the friendship. Second, knowledge of Torah and its important wisdom and guidance is not in our genetic makeup, nor can we inherit it from those who have come before us. So we study this sacred text, wrestle with its contents, and make it our own. That way, not only can we cultivate a passion for Torah, but we can also pass it on to others. Finally, as we reach out to others, we remind ourselves that we do so in order to bring the presence of God into our midst—and into the lives of others.

PERSONAL REFLECTIONS

_____

_____

_____

_____

_____

This is what the Holy One said to Israel:
My children, what do I seek from you? I seek no
more than that you love one another and honor
one another.

—*Tana d'be Eliahu* 26

*W*e have learned a great deal about love and honor during the entire process of mourning. Now we are ready to express what we have learned to others. And we begin with those closest to us: the members of our families and friends who have supported and nurtured us during these past months. But we don't stop there. We express ourselves to those we don't know quite so well: acquaintances, business associates, even service personnel who make our lives just a little bit easier. But we don't stop there either. We express ourselves even to strangers, even to beggars on the street. As we honor others, we honor our Maker, as well.

PERSONAL REFLECTIONS

_____

_____

_____

_____

_____

---

*It shall be due from the Israelites for all time
throughout the ages.*

—Exodus 27:21

*T*his text from Exodus refers to the requirement of Israelites to provide oil for the ancient Temple in Jerusalem. By doing so, all the Israelites contributed by bringing their own light into the sacred precincts. The priests would then consecrate the oil for religious purposes. While it was a specific directive, the notion can be extended beyond the context of the Temple. As Jews, we have responsibilities to the Jewish community and our fellow Jews. The Talmud teaches us that we are all responsible for one another. This is part of our covenantal responsibility. And so we reach out to others, and we open ourselves to their acts of kindness, as well. This is a perfect system if we all participate in it.

PERSONAL REFLECTIONS

_____

_____

_____

_____

_____

_____

The work of charity shall convey peace.
—Isaiah 32:17

*I*n the midst of the tumultuous ancient world, Isaiah knew that he had to bring a message of hope and peace to the world. In that respect, things have not changed very much since his time, the eighth century B.C.E. In our mourning, we long for the same message. Maybe the prophet should have said it another way: The work of charity *is* to convey peace. As we reach out to others at their time of need, we bring peace to them and to ourselves. And in doing so, we increase peace in the world. All it takes is the willingness to act. Rabbi Hillel framed it this way: "The more righteousness (*tzedakah*), the more peace" (*Pirke Avot* 2:7).

PERSONAL REFLECTIONS

_____

_____

_____

_____

_____

_____

_____

A Meditation
Before Saying Kaddish

Our sorrow can bring understanding as well as pain, breadth as well as the contraction that comes with pain. Out of love and sorrow can come a compassion that endures. The needs of others hitherto unnoticed, the anxieties of neighbors never before realized, now come into the ken of our experience, for our sorrow has opened our life to the needs of others.

Sorrow can enlarge the domain of our life, so that we may now understand the triviality of the things many pursue. What is important is not luxury but love; not wealth but wisdom; not gold but goodness.

And our sorrow may clear our vision so that we may, more brightly, see the God of whom it was said, "The Lord is nigh unto them that are of a broken heart." Beyond the hurry and turmoil of life rises the Eternal. There is a God in a world in which human beings could experience tenderness. There is a God in a world in which two lives can be bound together by a tie stronger than death.

Out of love may come sorrow; but out of sorrow can come light for others who dwell in darkness. And out of the light we bring others will come light for ourselves—the light of solace, of strength, of transfiguring and consecrating purpose.

—Morris Adler

Extending Ourselves

Sunday/Yom Rishon _____ (today's date)

*This is the blessing with which Moses, the one of
God, bade the Israelites farewell. . . .*
—Deuteronomy 33:1

*T*his verse introduces Moses' final message to the Israelites as they are about to cross over the Jordan River into Canaan. Read in synagogue always on Simchat Torah, it is recited as we conclude Torah study in anticipation of beginning once again. Every time we read Torah, we gain new insights and understandings for our lives. Usually we think of this ritual as a special way of concluding the reading of the Torah and then beginning it once again. But Moses' blessing to the people may, in fact, be contained in the ritual: This reflects renewal that is contained in the Torah. This is similar to the Israelites on their journey who thought that it was they who carried the Torah, while it was the Torah that carried them.

PERSONAL REFLECTIONS

_____

_____

_____

_____

_____

> *All beginnings require that you*
> *unlock new doors.*
> *The key is giving and doing.*
> *Give charity and do kindness.*
> —Rebbe Nachman of Breslov, *Likutey Moharan* II:4,
> quoted in *The Empty Chair*

*A*s each door closes behind us, a new one opens in front of us. This is the reality we have faced in mourning. But we have to be courageous enough to enter that new door. It is not easy. It takes time. We may want to run back and try to force the old door open. Some people bang on that door real hard. This is of no use. Death keeps the door to the past closed to us. So how do we cause that new door to stay open? Rebbe Nachman teaches that the key is through giving *tzedakah* (charitable giving) and doing *gemilut chasadim* (loving acts of kindness). If we do this, we will soon find that a thousand doors will fling open as a result of such activity.

PERSONAL REFLECTIONS

_____

_____

_____

_____

_____

How does one love God? By encompassing oneself with benevolence on every side, by doing benevolence to all without sparing one's strength or property.

—*Zohar* V, 267a

It is not enough to study Torah and learn from its teachings. We have to find ways to actually *become* the Torah by modeling its instructions and wisdom in everything that we do. This is particularly true in the ways we now reach out to others, as they have done to us these past months of mourning. We may feel too emotionally drained at first to reach out to other mourners, especially while we are still mourning. Yet, you can reach down into the reservoir of inner strength that remains hidden inside the soul. By reaching out to others, your strength will not wane. The opposite is true. You are the one who is strengthened when you spread the love of God to others. So just go out and *be* Torah.

PERSONAL REFLECTIONS

_____

_____

_____

_____

_____

> *There are ten hard things in the world.*
> —Babylonian Talmud, *Bava Batra* 10a

Only ten? The rabbis don't really specify. I imagine that they think that we all have our own lists. In any case, each of us probably has a list longer than ten. And that list might not even match what the rabbis would suggest. We would probably all agree, however, that experiencing the loss of a loved one is at the top of the list. There is nothing more difficult in this world than facing the death of others. But we were not given a choice about this. As hard as it is to mourn, it is even harder to conclude the prescribed period of mourning because we have to let go of a daily connection with our deceased. So we ease out of mourning by helping others who are just beginning to mourn.

PERSONAL REFLECTIONS

_____

_____

_____

_____

_____

_____

Thursday/Yom Chamishi _____ (today's date)

Rabbi Nehunye ben Hakana used to offer the following prayer upon entering the Bet Midrash *[House of Study] and upon exiting it. . . . Upon entering, I pray that I will not bring harm to anyone in my teaching and upon leaving, I thank God for my lot.*
—Babylonian Talmud, *Berakhot* 28b

It takes a great deal of faith to be as concerned about others as was Rabbi Nehunye. He knew that his words might be misconstrued—even when he spoke words of Torah. He was careful about what he taught and to whom. As we have learned in mourning—and as we are still learning—it takes even greater faith to thank God for our lot, recognizing what has befallen us. But the key to this rabbi's profound religious faith is contained in the first line of his prayer. Regardless of what happened to him, he continued to teach words of Torah. It is that teaching that gave the rabbi the strength to thank God, regardless of his lot. We express our thanks to God by sharing what we have learned with others.

PERSONAL REFLECTIONS

_____

_____

_____

_____

*I will not go [with you on your journey] but will
return to my native land.*

—Numbers 10:30

*M*oses' father-in-law Jethro helped Moses determine how to lead the people. Some scholars even suggest that Jethro helped Moses clarify his faith in the one true God. After spending a great deal of time advising Moses, Jethro returned home to Midian when he thought that Moses was ready to carry on on his own. And the Israelites, led by Moses and Miriam, continued on their journey. Sometimes we have to do what Jethro did. We may offer others words of comfort and advice and suggestions about how to continue living—just like others have offered to us—and then we must return home and reestablish our lives. We must continue on the journey alone—and let others do the same.

PERSONAL REFLECTIONS

_____

_____

_____

_____

_____

_____

Saturday/Shabbat _____ (today's date)

> *For Zion's sake, I will not be silent,*
> *For Jerusalem's sake, I will not be still.*
>
> —Isaiah 62:1

*S*ometimes it feels easier not to say or do anything to help other people bear their burdens. Why not just leave people alone to face their own challenges in life? We think to ourselves, perhaps they will do the same with us. But we know that it is not the case. People, in fact, continue to ask about our well-being. They will do so even months after the initial period of mourning is over. Following the teachings of prophets like Isaiah, Jewish tradition teaches us to reach out to one another, to raise our voices in protest or in song. For the sake of Zion, for the sake of Jerusalem, and for your own sake, we cannot be silent or still. We must speak out and be heard so that we may all listen to the echo of God's voice in our words.

PERSONAL REFLECTIONS

_____

_____

_____

_____

_____

_____

A Meditation
Before Saying Kaddish

⎯⎯⎯ ⟳⟳⟳ ⎯⎯⎯

We attempt to help souls rise up after a death. To facilitate the ascent of the soul of a close relative, a *neshamah*, or soul light, is kindled on the anniversary (Yahrzeit) of the death, and also on the Day of Atonement, when even souls of the departed are judged anew and when Yizkor, the Prayer for Remembrance, is said. The Kaddish said during mourning is a parallel means of elevating the soul through words rather than lights. The actual words that begin the Kaddish are "raise up" and exalt God, but in doing so on behalf of the dead who can no longer speak for himself, the soul itself is raised. . . .

—*Adapted from* FREEMA GOTTLIEB

Providing Counsel

And the priest shall offer the burnt offering and
the meal offering on the altar, and make
expiation for the individual to be made clean.

—Leviticus 14:20

This verse is taken from a section of the Torah that most people prefer to avoid. We would rather that Torah only shine with Divine light rather than also reveal the dark sides of life. But then Torah would not reflect the full human experience as it does. This part of Leviticus deals primarily with various kinds of infections and how to get rid of them. Modern medicine may take issue with some of its procedures. However, it is interesting to note that the priest cures the ill person through an elaborate process that includes first taking the burden onto himself. The priests realized something that we have also learned through mourning: We lighten each other's burdens by sharing them with others.

PERSONAL REFLECTIONS

_____

_____

_____

_____

_____

Grant Your servant a heart that hears.

—1 Kings 3:9

$\mathcal{I}$n order to help others, we have to listen attentively to them. This takes a hearing heart. We also have to listen to people even when they don't want to talk. Even silence speaks. During this mourning period, we may not have been listening to others very much. Instead, we were listening more to the cries of anguish of our own soul. But now, as our mourning nears conclusion, we have to be willing to listen to others. When the Israelites received the Torah at Mount Sinai, they said, *"Naaseh venishmah—* We will do and we will hear"* (Deuteronomy 5:24). They knew what we have learned: Doing includes careful, attentive listening. When we listen to the voice of others, we hear God's voice calling out to us, as well.

PERSONAL REFLECTIONS

_____

_____

_____

_____

_____

_____

_____

Harachaman, *Merciful One,*
open the gates of your wondrous storehouse
releasing your sparkling dew. . . .
Droplets of dew, come gently,
fetching a year of goodness,
filling with peace the reservoir of my soul.
—Rabbi Nina Beth Cardin

In the heat of the summer, soon after Pesach, when the rains no longer fall in Israel, the land becomes arid. In anticipation of this extensive dryness, we regularly ask God to send dew to moisten the parched earth. We invite God to nurture the plants that depend on this heaven-sent water for life. Even those of us who do not live on the land make this request, since, by doing so, we also ask God to water our arid souls and bring nourishment to our parched life. In anticipation of the year ahead, we ask God to send us such dew so that we, too, may live. Nurtured by these redemptive waters, we know that we can carry God's message of hope to others.

PERSONAL REFLECTIONS

_____

_____

_____

_____

Wednesday/Yom Revii _____ (today's date)

The hoary head is a crown of glory.
—Proverbs 16:31

*M*ourning ages an individual. Some say that losing a parent turns a child into an adult. As we have learned, mourning also reminds us of our own mortality, particularly as we become the senior members of our family. Jewish tradition prides itself on the potential wisdom that can come from the experience of aging. And the deaths of those we love become more frequent as we grow older. In North America, we often try to cover up any signs of growing older. Perhaps we want to prove to others that we are still young, vital, with much life ahead of us. But gray hair and wrinkled skin are signs of life, not death. Wear them proudly.

PERSONAL REFLECTIONS

_____

_____

_____

_____

_____

_____

_____

Thursday/Yom Chamishi _____ (today's date)

The one who speaks of worldly matters and
religious matters as if they are distinct is a heretic.
—The Baal Shem Tov

$\mathcal{T}$ired of what he perceived as the intellectualization of Judaism, Rabbi Israel ben Eliezer founded the Hasidic movement in the eighteenth century and became known as the Baal Shem Tov, literally "The Master of the Good Name." He earned this name as one who possessed secret knowledge about the unpronounceable four-letter Name of God. The Baal Shem Tov taught by telling stories and doing good deeds for others. During his travels, he shared his love for Judaism and the Jewish people. He told stories about his own life and religious struggles, never separating the real world from religious values. We can follow the Baal Shem Tov's example. By doing so, we can become masters of God's Name in our own day.

PERSONAL REFLECTIONS

And the two of them walked on together.
—Genesis 22:8b

On their way to Mount Moriah, Abraham and Isaac "walked together." In their own way, each met the challenge of the mountain together, the challenge of what our tradition calls the "binding of Isaac." Even after our mourning is over, we realize that there will be many other challenges to be faced in our lives. And that we will have to face them. As painful as this time has been, mourning has prepared us to meet future challenges. And now, we will meet them together with others who face the same struggles as we do. And we will teach others what we have learned: None of us is ever alone—and there is nothing that God and we cannot handle together.

PERSONAL REFLECTIONS

_____

_____

_____

_____

_____

_____

_____

I will give you a new heart;
and a new spirit will I put in you;
I will remove the heart of stone from your body,
and give you a heart of flesh.
—Ezekiel 36:26

*A*fter these many months of mourning, we seem to be drained of all emotion. Throughout the mourning process, it often felt as if we had been on an emotional roller coaster. We may have cried or laughed unexpectedly and without any particular reason. Our friends and members of our family may have been uncomfortable with our unpredictable behavior. They were careful what they said to us and maybe even limited their interaction with us. And then after a while, perhaps we felt no emotion at all. That is why Ezekiel's promise to us offers hope and inspiration, particularly as we ready ourselves to now reach out to others. With a "heart of flesh," we can experience joy once again. We *can* learn to live anew.

PERSONAL REFLECTIONS

_____

_____

_____

_____

_____

A Meditation
Before Saying Kaddish

⚬⟋⟍⟋⟍⚬

The external meaning of words alone cannot move us. It is the inward flame of devotion that brings our prayers close to God. Indeed, as the Hebrew phrasing vividly conveys, a passionate longing for godliness can exist among those unable to express that feeling in words. The phrase *lahav tefilatam*, "the flame of Israel's prayers," reaches that feeling of *hitlahavut*, the in-burning flame of passionate devotion. To attain *hitlahavut* in prayer is to soar to the rapturous ecstasy of divine communion, to access the infinite and be aflame with the nearness of God.
—ARTHUR GREEN *and* RABBI MARCIA PRAEGER

Elevating the Spirit

Sunday/Yom Rishon _____ (today's date)

> *Be on guard about everything*
> *that I have told you.*
> —Based on Leviticus 19:37

During mourning, we often listen to a lot of advice from others. Well-meaning people want to tell us what to do to "get over" our loss or "get through" our mourning. They may have shared their own experiences with grief with us, hoping that we may learn from what they experienced. But there is no way to avoid confronting the pain of grief ourselves. Now toward the end of the mourning process, we have the opportunity to reflect on everything that we have heard. We have to search for truth in the many words that have been spoken. We also have to be careful not to reject the important things that might have been said. So we look for the word of God in the voice of friends.

PERSONAL REFLECTIONS

_____

_____

_____

_____

_____

_____

> *When a scroll of the Law is sewn together it*
> *becomes holy, and it is forbidden*
> *to erase a letter in it.*
> —Rabbi Levi Yitzchak of Berditchev

*M*any of the rules that govern the writing of a Torah scroll reflect profound spiritual teachings. That is why teachers like Levi Yitzchak bring them to our attention. It seems that before the sections of a scroll are sewn together, some erasure is allowed. But once the scroll is sewn together, it is considered holy. A Torah can be repaired, and whole sections can be replaced, but nothing can be erased on it. Apparently, *kedushah*, holiness, is a result of sewing together. Similarly, when individuals come together in the context of forming a Jewish community, it becomes holy. As we reach out to others—and permit them to reach out to us—we help to create this holiness. The attainment of holiness is within our reach.

PERSONAL REFLECTIONS

_____

_____

_____

_____

_____

> *Ben Azzai said, "Despise no one and consider*
> *nothing as impossible for there is not a person*
> *who does not have his or her hour and not a*
> *thing that does not have its place."*
> —*Pirke Avot* 4:3

𝒲e ask ourselves, "Do we have the strength to continue our lives in the same way we did before we became mourners—and also help others who are in mourning?" Simeon ben Azzai, who lived in Tiberias in the early second century B.C.E., reminds us that while it may be difficult to do so and there may be obstacles in our way, we will be able to do it. Surely, we will encounter people who will make the transition out of mourning difficult. They may remind us of the pain of our loss while we are trying to find ways to lessen it. But we have to remember that it was a stranger who steered the biblical Joseph to find his brothers, that this person whom he simply encountered on the road gave him directions for his life.

PERSONAL REFLECTIONS

_____

_____

_____

_____

_____

The one who walks with the wise shall be wise.
—Proverbs 13:20

This passage from Proverbs is yet another version of a basic rule we learned in childhood. Like so many basic truths we learned in our youth, it sustains us in adulthood: The company we keep is important. Peers influence our outlook on life; they influence who we become and who we are. So the wisdom of this proverb is simple. If we want to gain wisdom and insight from our days of mourning so we can share it with others, then we should find wise people from whom we can learn. Joshua ben Perachya, a scholar from the second century B.C.E. said it this way: "Get yourself a teacher and find yourself a friend with whom to study" (*Pirke Avot* 1:6). This kind of wisdom will preserve us.

PERSONAL REFLECTIONS

_____

_____

_____

_____

_____

_____

_____

God kissed Moses and took away his soul with a
kiss of the mouth. Then God wept.
—*Midrash Petirat Moshe*

*E*xperiencing the death of those we love is part of the raw experience of living. No matter how many times we repeat this notion to ourselves, it does not make affirming it any easier. We don't like to acknowledge death as part of reality, but it is something that we are forced to learn again and again. Even Moses, the greatest teacher in Jewish history, died without being able to fulfill his lifelong ambition: to see the Promised Land and take our people into it. The rabbis of the midrash, troubled by Moses' disappointment, imagined that God tended to Moses' death directly. Yet, we all die the same way—with God's kiss lingering on our lips, salty from the shedding of Divine tears.

PERSONAL REFLECTIONS

_____

_____

_____

_____

_____

_____

Come now and I will send you to Pharaoh.
—Exodus 3:10

*M*oses was diffident about going to see Pharaoh when God asked him to do so. Just like all of us when we have to do something about which we are hesitant, Moses came up with a dozen excuses. But God addressed each concern. God even invited Aaron to accompany Moses, as much to bolster his confidence as to provide Moses with a spokesperson who was not "heavy of tongue." Even after mourning for so many months, we are hesitant about reaching out to others, especially those who are just beginning to also mourn for a recent death. We feel like we don't know what to say or do. But the best advice is often the simplest. And so, if you speak from the depth of your experience, your feeling heart will do the rest.

PERSONAL REFLECTIONS

_____

_____

_____

_____

_____

_____

_____

Saturday/Shabbat _____ (today's date)

The sun shall no more go down
Neither shall the moon withdraw itself
For Adonai will be your everlasting light
And the days of your mourning will be ended.
—Isaiah 60:20

*A*t the end of our mourning, the prophet offers us a *nechemta*, words of consolation that lift the spirit. God makes this promise to us just as God made the promise to the ancient Israelites through the prophet Isaiah. For the remainder of our days on earth, we will be able to depend on the orderliness of the world and the light of God to illumine our path as we make our way through it. You have changed since you first began to mourn. You have learned many things about life, about others, about yourself. You can now get up from your mourning and reestablish your life knowing full well that when you falter, God will be there to lift you up once again.

PERSONAL REFLECTIONS

_____

_____

_____

_____

_____

A Meditation
Before Saying Kaddish

᠊ᠣᠰᠣᠣ᠊

May we live unselfishly, in truth and love and peace, so that we will be remembered as a blessing, as we this day lovingly remember those whose lives endure as a blessing.

Our generations are bound to each other as children now remember their parents. Love is as strong as death as husbands and wives now remember their mates, as parents now remember their children. Memory conquers death's dominion as we now remember our brothers and sisters, grandparents and other relatives and friends.

The death of those we now remember left gaping holes in our lives. But we are grateful for the gift of their lives. And we are strengthened by the blessing they left us, by precious memories which comfort and sustain us as we recall them this day.

—*Mahzor for Rosh Hashanah and Yom Kippur*

What to Do When You Conclude Saying Kaddish

Most people say Kaddish for eleven months rather than the twelve months that might be anticipated by "a year of mourning." At the end of the twelfth month, we say Kaddish once again to mark the *yahrzeit* anniversary of our loved one's death. By stopping at the end of eleven months, we have thirty days to help us prepare concluding the formal first year of mourning. But we don't just stop saying Kaddish and then start our lives again as if nothing transpired. Our lives have changed drastically over the course of these eleven months. And we have to acknowledge that transition. We are not the same individuals that we once were. Much has transpired. And we have grown accustomed to the regular routine of saying Kaddish each day which must now change. Just as we began shiva with a prescribed Jewish ritual choreography, it is important to similarly mark the end of the period of saying Kaddish. This pattern of Jewish mourning reflects the rhythm of our lives.

While patterns of observance have evolved differently in various communities, you might do one or more of the following to formally mark the end of the period of saying Kaddish.

- Join the local minyan on a Torah-reading day and request an *aliyah* (Torah honor). If you are able to do so, prepare to read from the Torah. An "old country" tradition is to bring some pound cake and schnapps to share after the service.

- Make a *tzedakah* contribution to honor the memory of your loved one. Instead of mailing the check, bring it to the organization yourself. Or, better yet, volunteer your time that day to help the organization.

- Arrange for the unveiling of the gravestone, if you have not already done so in previous months.

- Visit the cemetery. Say Kaddish at graveside to conclude the month. You may want to include the *El Maleh Rachamin* prayer. Leave a stone on the grave marker.

- Join the early morning study group at a local synagogue. Arrange to teach a lesson in the memory of your loved one, even something small. Perhaps you can teach something that you learned from him or her.

For the Weeks and Years That Follow Your Mourning

Yahrzeit

Like the Kaddish, the *Yahrzeit* (anniversary of a death) is a powerful magnet, drawing a man back to the synagogue and back to his people with regular and incessant rhythm. Even those whose synagogue affiliations are slender make new contact on this memory-hallowed day. Even in small communities, where there is no regular minyan and where the house of prayer is closed the entire week, even there the doors of the synagogue are opened and arrangements are made for a service to take place when a Jew has a *Yahrzeit* to observe. For the observance of the *Yahrzeit* is one of the honors that a man can pay his departed parents, and it is a duty that his heart, mind, and conscience bid him pay with scrupulous care. As the strains of the *Yahrzeit* reverberate through his soul, they reawaken with indescribable poignancy the faded memories of past years.

—Rabbi Tzvi Rabinowicz

Yizkor

Yizkor [memorial prayers said during holidays] is for letting the music come back, softly and sweetly. *Yizkor* is to hush us and to heal us, because we are very tired under the burden which death has brought. *Yizkor* is to hush us with the quiet strength of prayer. *Yizkor* is to heal us with the wisdom that death gives urgency to life. Then sit quiet, without bitter tears, and let the silence flow in, bringing more love than grief, more gratitude than rebellion.

—Rabbi Jacob Philip Rudin

Holiday and Festival Reflections

Rosh Hashanah

> *You will cast all of your sins into the depths*
> *of the sea, and may You cast all of the sins of*
> *Your people, the house of Israel, into a place*
> *where they shall be no more remembered*
> *or visited or ever come to mind.*
>
> —From the *Tashlikh* ceremony

It is perhaps during the fall holy days that we miss our deceased most intensely. The summer is over, and it is time for families to get together. The place usually filled by our loved one is empty. Many thoughts linger from our months of mourning, and the hours we sit in the synagogue offer us the opportunity to think about them. The blasts of the shofar raise us above our complacency and encourage us to confront these things head-on. They may be things that we thought about that needed resolution with the deceased while he or she was alive. And we realize now that it is no longer possible. And so we look to the *Tashlikh* ceremony, during which time we symbolically cast our sins into the water, to offer us comfort. In many areas of North America, the fall winds are blowing, the temperatures are cooling, and the leaves may even have already begun to change their colors as the trees prepare for winter. As we symbolically cast our sins from the past year into the waters, we also cast with it the many issues and conflicts that may have gone unresolved prior to the death of our loved one. Here and now we make a commitment to ourselves and to God that while the memories of our loved ones remain forever alive, the unresolved issues are gone, never to be resurfaced again. We pray: May we be inscribed this year for a new year that is sweet and tranquil, filled with promises and new beginnings.

Yom Kippur

> *Yom Kippur atones for transgressions against God, but it does not atone for transgressions of one human being against another unless we have made peace with one another.*
> —*Mishnah Yoma* 8:9

Yom Kippur brings to an end the High Holiday season. This introspective period really began with the Hebrew month of Elul, some 30 days prior to Rosh Hashanah, during which time we reflect on Psalm 27 each day and also ask forgiveness directly from people we have wronged. On Yom Kippur, we face God more directly than at any time of the year, perhaps even more directly than our most intense periods of self-reflection during the entire mourning process. Recognizing the religious intensity of the experience, we especially now long for our loved one. We may miss our loved one most now because we remember the many hours sitting next to them in synagogue. Or perhaps of a particular conversation that we had with them as a result of the process of *cheshbon hanefesh*, the self-accounting, that Yom Kippur enjoins upon us. Whatever is the case, we certainly feel their absence now. And as we enter the synagogue as we do each year in order to stand before God for judgment, thinking back over the deeds and misdeeds of the previous year, we know that we stand strengthened by the memory of our deceased. They stand with us in spirit, as they do wherever life takes us. And we feel comforted and confident that the year ahead will be a good one.

Sukkot

You shall dwell in booths.

—Leviticus 23:42

For many generations, Jews have been building the thatched booths in which they live during the week of Sukkot. These duplicate the portable dwelling places that our ancestors built during their wandering in the desert. In the modern world of city-dwelling, we may not know much about farming, but we sure know a lot about wandering. The sukkahs also remind us of the huts that our forebears built during harvest season so that they could get respite from the sun while out in the fields for the entire harvest season. In both cases, these structures were temporary and portable and could be moved from place to place. And they were fragile much like we are, now that we are recent mourners. Sukkot teaches about the fragility of life, but it also teaches about the reservoir of inner strength in the men and women who made the desert journey. It even reminds us of their occasional failures and disillusionments. Ultimately, Sukkot reminds us that life—particularly after our year of mourning—is itself a journey. As we dwell in the sukkah, we become those men and women of strength. The sukkah reminds us that we are not alone, that God will guide us through the desert and ultimately into the Promised Land. So why build a sukkah? Simply put, it brings us closer to God—and closer to our original selves.

Hanukkah

> *A great miracle happened* here.
> —Inscription on Israeli dreidels

The presence of our loved one is missed during the joyous celebration of Hanukkah. Families get together. They light candles on *hanukiyot*, Hanukkah menorahs, and exchange recipes for crispy, tasty latkes, potato pancakes. We celebrate as if someone is not missing, but we realize that our loved one is indeed absent. Most dreidels are inscribed: A great miracle happened *there*, referring to the Land of Israel where Judah and his small band of Maccabees defeated the mighty Syrian-Greek armies that threatened the land. More significantly, these foreign armies threatened the Jewish way of life. The ancient Israelites learned the lesson of Zechariah (which is read as the haftarah for *Shabbat Hanukkah*), just as we have learned it during our mourning: It is "'not by might, nor by power, but by My spirit,' says God" (Zechariah 4:6). But the world is too small for two different dreidels, one in Israel and one elsewhere, for the miracles of "those days in years past" as the *Al Hanissim* prayer phrases it,

Hanukkah miracles happen to us right *here*. Sure, there are many things that continue to threaten our faith, particularly after a year of mourning. But we have now opened ourselves up to the everyday miracles that we previously had not recognized when we took life for granted. And so we pray: May a great miracle happen to us all, here and now.

Purim

With the beginning of Adar we make joy.
—Babylonian Talmud, *Taanit* 29a

Purim is an upside-down festival. We treat even the most sacred in Judaism with a large dose of loving disrespect. We make all kinds of noise in the synagogue as the biblical scroll of Esther is read aloud. Our teachers are mocked in good spirit in the Purim *shpiel*, a satirical Purim play, and we hide our true selves behind masks of the season. It is one big day of celebration. There is even controversy over the real intention of the talmudic injunction to drink until we cannot tell the difference between the phrase "Blessed be Mordecai and cursed be Haman." This is one festival that our tradition goes to great lengths to find ways to make us happy. In fact, we seem to have no real choice in the matter. In ancient Persia, our ancestors were doomed, yet they survived. We mourn the death of one we love, and after a year of mourning, we too are survivors. It is difficult to be happy when our emotions still tell us otherwise. But we have to listen to the wisdom of our tradition. For this month, which is epitomized by the festival of Purim, we will forget the pain that remains embedded in our soul. And we will teach others the one main lesson that this month has to offer: Be happy; it's Adar.

Pesach

> *In every generation, it is incumbent upon the*
> *individual to consider oneself personally*
> *delivered from Egypt.*
>
> —Haggadah

Every year as we sit around the dining room table for the Passover Seder, we review the story of our ancestors' journey from Egyptian slavery to freedom. I like to sit comfortably in the living room or family room and retell the story in a really relaxed way. Regardless of how well we know the story, the Haggadah reminds us: "Now even if all of us were scholars, all of us were sages, all of us elders, all of us learned in Torah, it still would be our duty to tell the story of the Exodus from Egypt." We have to go over the story time and time again so that we remember it. Moreover, we tell the story so that we will not forget it. For it is our experience as well as the experience of our ancestors. And with the storytelling come family memories. Each family has them. Customs also emerge and become part of the family tradition that gets carried to the next year. We all have our own. And as we sit around the table, we are mindful of those who are not with us. So we remind ourselves of their impact on our lives by sharing our Passover memories of them. Just as we set aside a cup of wine for Elijah, we also set aside an empty chair that is filled with memory of our beloved. This year, we remember—and we will do so again next year, as well.

Shavuot

Entreat me not to leave you, for wherever you go, I will go . . .

—Ruth 1:16

The winter rains are over in the land of Israel. Spring has emerged full-blossomed from the dark dormancy of winter. And we join together once again as a community to consider the many blessings that we share. Several themes merge into one on Shavuot. While Shavuot is the spring harvest festival on which the ancients brought their first fruits to the Temple in Jerusalem, it also focuses on the revelation of Torah to the Jewish people on Mount Sinai. Moreover, Shavuot speaks to the many people who, during the course of Jewish history, have decided to throw in their lot with ours. This is epitomized by Ruth's words to her mother-in-law Naomi that are quoted above. The biblical scroll of Ruth is read during Shavuot. While these powerful sentiments speak to all of us, they are particularly poignant to us as recent mourners. We know that wherever we go and whatever we do with our lives from this day forward, we will carry our memories of our beloved with us. While they are no longer with us in the physical world, we are never without their spirit. And it is their spirit that buoys us and sustains us.

Notes

Denying Death

p. 10   Lawrence Kushner, *Invisible Lines of Connection: Sacred Stories of the Ordinary* (Woodstock, Vt.: Jewish Lights Publishing, 1996).

p. 18   Harold Kushner, *When Bad Things Happen to Good People* (New York: Schocken Books, 1989).

The Disorganization of My Life

p. 40   Rebbe Nachman of Breslov, *The Empty Chair: Finding Hope and Joy* (Woodstock, Vt.: Jewish Lights Publishing, 1994); adapted by Moshe Mykoff and the Breslov Research Institute.

p. 55   *Reform Judaism* 23, no. 2 (Winter 1994): 2.

p. 64   Joshua Loth Liebman, *Peace of Mind* (New York: Simon & Schuster, 1946).

Directing My Anger

p. 85   Lawrence Kushner, *The River of Light: Spirituality, Judaism, Consciousness* (Woodstock, Vt.: Jewish Lights Publishing, 1990).

p. 111   John D. Rayner and Chaim Stern, eds., *Siddur Lev Chadash* (London: Union of Liberal and Progressive Synagogues, 1995); adapted from Chaim Stern, ed., *Gates of Prayer* (New York: Central Conference of American Rabbis, 1975).

Feeling Guilty and Making Deals

p. 148   Chaim Stern, ed., *Gates of Prayer.*

Out of the Depths I Call to You

p. 152   *Likutei Moharan* 1:8, quoted in Rebbe Nachman of Breslov, *The Empty Chair: Finding Hope and Joy* (Woodstock, Vt.: Jewish Lights Publishing, 1994); adapted by Moshe Mykoff and the Breslov Research Institute.

p. 152   These psalms are available in translation with commentary in Simkha Y. Weintraub, ed., *Healing of Soul, Healing of Body: Spiritual Leaders Unfold the Strength & Solace in Psalms* (Woodstock, Vt.: Jewish Lights Publishing, 1994).

p. 159   Joshua Loth Liebman, Sermon, Message of Israel, n.d.

Introspection

p. 196   Austin Kutscher, ed., *Religion and Bereavement* (New York: Health Sciences Publishing Corporation, 1972).

p. 213   Bennett Miller, ed., *Purify Our Hearts: A Prayer Book for Sabbath Morning* (New Brunswick, N.J.: Anshe Emeth Memorial Temple, n.d.).

p. 221   Peter Gossels and Nancy Gossels, eds., *Vetaher Libenu* (Sudbury, Mass.: Temple Beth El of the Sudbury River Valley, 1992).

Feeling Isolated and Alone

p. 232   Sidney Greenberg, *Words to Live by: Selected Writings* (Northvale, N.J.: Jason Aronson, 1990).

p. 240   Diana Bletter and Lori Grinker, eds., *The Invisible Thread: A Portrait of Jewish American Women* (Philadelphia: The Jewish Publication Society of America, 1989).

p. 256   Gerson B. Levi, *The Thanksgiving of the Spirit and Other Sermons* (Chicago: Argus Book Store, 1938).

Withdrawing from the Past

p. 266   Sidney Greenberg, *Words to Live By: Selected Writings.*

p. 271   Rebbe Nachman of Breslov, *The Empty Chair: Finding Hope and Joy* (Woodstock, Vt.: Jewish Lights Publishing, 1994); adapted by Moshe Mykoff and the Breslov Research Institute.

p. 276   Jakob Petuchowski, *Understanding Jewish Prayer* (New York: KTAV, 1972).

p. 283   Chaim Stern, ed., *Gates of Prayer.*

p. 292   Anne Brener, *Mourning & Mitzvah: A Guided Journal for Walking the Mourner's Path Through Grief to Healing* (Woodstock, Vt.: Jewish Lights Publishing, 1993).

Coming to Accept

p. 296   *Union Prayer Book* (New York: Central Conference of American Rabbis, 1922).

p. 302   Joshua Loth Liebman, *Peace of Mind.*

p. 307   Anne Brener, *Mourning & Mitzvah: A Guided Journal for Walking the Mourner's Path through Grief to Healing* (Woodstock, Vt.: Jewish Lights Publishing, 1993).

p. 310   Lawrence Kushner, *The River of Light: Spirituality, Judaism, Consciousness* (Woodstock, Vt.: Jewish Lights Publishing, 1990).

p. 312   Morris Raphael Cohen, *A Dreamer's Journey: Autobiography of Morris Raphael Cohen* (Boston: Beacon Press, 1949).

p. 314   Neil Gillman, *The Death of Death: Resurrection and Immortality in Jewish Thought* (Woodstock, Vt.: Jewish Lights Publishing, 1997).

p. 315   Jack Riemer, *Jewish Reflections on Death* (New York: Schocken Books, 1976).

p. 322   Abraham Joshua Heschel, *Man's Quest for God* (New York: Macmillan, 1981).

p. 325   Deena Metzger, *A Sabbath Among the Ruins* (Berkeley: Paulist Press, 1992).

The Path Toward Healing

p. 331   Rebbe Nachman of Breslov, *The Empty Chair: Finding Hope and Joy* (Woodstock, Vt.: Jewish Lights Publishing, 1994); adapted by Moshe Mykoff and the Breslov Research Institute.

p. 333   Menachem Mendel of Kotzk, *Emet VeEmunah*.

p. 338   Moses Maimonides, *Thirteen Principles of Faith*.

p. 339   Eugene B. Borowitz, *The Centenary Perspective* (New York: Central Conference of American Rabbis, 1976).

p. 344   Jacob K. Shankman, "Remembrance," in *Religion and Bereavement*, ed. Austin Kutscher.

p. 347   Commentary to Proverbs 28.

p. 359   Sheldon Zimmerman, "A Prayer for Prayer," *Healing of Soul, Healing of Body: Spiritual Leaders Unfold the Strength & Solace in Psalms*, ed. Simkha Y. Weintraub (Woodstock, Vt.: Jewish Lights Publishing, 1994), 102.

Reaching Out to Others

p. 364   Felix Adler, *Creed and Deed* (New York: G. P. Putnam's Sons, 1850), adapted.

p. 371   Morris Adler, *May I Have a Word with You* (New York: Crown Publishers, 1967).

p. 373   Rebbe Nachman of Breslov, *The Empty Chair: Finding Hope and Joy* (Woodstock, Vt.: Jewish Lights Publishing, 1994); adapted by Moshe Mykoff and the Breslov Research Institute.

p. 379   Freema Gottlieb, *The Lamp of God* (Northvale, N.J.: Jason Aronson, 1989).

p. 387   *Kol Haneshamah* (Wyncote, Penn.: Reconstructionist Press, 1989).

p. 395   *Mahzor for Rosh Hashanah and Yom Kippur* (New York: Rabbinical Assembly, 1972).

For the Weeks and Years That Follow Your Mourning

p. 399   Tzvi Rabinowicz, *A Guide to Life* (Northvale, N.J.: Jason Aronson, 1989).

p. 400   Jacob Philip Rudin, "Remembrance," in *Religion and Bereavement*, ed. Austin Kutscher.

About the Author

Rabbi Kerry M. Olitzky, D.H.L., is National Dean of Adult Jewish Learning and Living at Hebrew Union College–Jewish Institute of Religion. At the forefront of Jewish education, he is the organizer of many programs on chemical dependency. Rabbi Olitzky is Special Issues Editor on Aging and Judaism for the *Journal of Psychology and Judaism*. He is Executive Editor of *Shofar* magazine and is Chair of the Editorial Committee of *Compass* magazine. He is the author of over 30 books and monographs and many articles on topics of Jewish interest.

About JEWISH LIGHTS Publishing

People of all faiths and backgrounds yearn for books that attract, engage, educate and spiritually inspire.

Our principal goal is to stimulate thought and help all people learn about who the Jewish People are, where they come from, and what the future can be made to hold. While people of our diverse Jewish heritage are the primary audience, our books speak to people in the Christian world as well and will broaden their understanding of Judaism and the roots of their own faith.

We bring to you authors who are at the forefront of spiritual thought and experience. While each has something different to say, they all say it in a voice that you can hear.

Our books are designed to welcome you and then to engage, stimulate and inspire. We judge our success not only by whether or not our books are beautiful and commercially successful, but by whether or not they make a difference in your life.

We at Jewish Lights take great care to produce beautiful books that present meaningful spiritual content in a form that reflects the art of making high quality books. Therefore, we want to acknowledge those who contributed to the production of this book.

EDITORIAL & PROOFREADING
Sandra Korinchak, Richard Fumosa, Jennifer Goneau

PRODUCTION
Maria O'Donnell

COVER DESIGN
Karen Savary, Deering, New Hampshire

BOOK DESIGN
Sans Serif, Saline, Michigan

COVER PRINTING
Phoenix Color Corp., Taunton, Massachusetts

PRINTING AND BINDING
Book Press, Brattleboro, Vermont

GRIEF IN OUR SEASONS
A Mourner's Kaddish Companion
by *Rabbi Kerry M. Olitzky*

Strength from the Jewish tradition for the first year of mourning.

Provides a wise and inspiring selection of sacred Jewish writings and a simple, powerful ancient ritual for mourners to read each day, to help hold the memory of their loved ones in their hearts. It offers a comforting, step-by-step daily link to saying *Kaddish*.

"A hopeful, compassionate guide along the journey from grief to rebirth from mourning to a new morning."
　　　　—*Rabbi Levi Meier, Ph.D., Chaplain, Cedars-Sinai Medical Center,*
　　　　　Los Angeles

4 1/2" x 6 1/2", 448 pp, Quality Paperback Original, ISBN 1-879045-55-9 **$15.95**

MOURNING MITZVAH
A Guided Journal for Walking the Mourner's Path Through Grief to Healing
by *Anne Brener, L.C.S.W.;*
Foreword by *Rabbi Jack Riemer;*
Introduction by *Rabbi William Cutter*

"Fully engaging in mourning means you will be a different person than before you began." For those who mourn a death, for those who would help them, for those who face a loss of any kind, Brener teaches us the power and strength available to us in the fully experienced mourning process. Guided writing exercises help stimulate the processes of both conscious and unconscious healing.

"A stunning book! It offers an exploration in depth of the place where psychology and religious ritual intersect, and the name of that place is Truth."
　　　　—*Rabbi Harold Kushner, author of* When Bad Things Happen
　　　　　to Good People

7 1/2" x 9", 288 pp. Quality Paperback Original, ISBN 1-879045-23-0 **$19.95**

WHEN A GRANDPARENT DIES
A Kid's Own Remembering Workbook for Dealing with Shiva and the Year Beyond
by *Nechama Liss-Levinson, Ph.D.*

Drawing insights from both psychology and Jewish tradition, this workbook helps children participate in the process of mourning, offering guided exercises, rituals, and places to write, draw, list, create and express their feelings.

"Will bring support, guidance, and understanding for countless children, teachers, and health professionals."
—*Rabbi Earl A. Grollman, D.D., author of* Talking about Death

8" x 10", 48 pp. HC, illus., 2-color text, ISBN 1-879045-44-3 **$15.95**

A TIME TO MOURN, A TIME TO COMFORT
A Guide to Jewish Bereavement and Comfort
by *Dr. Ron Wolfson*

A guide to meeting the needs of those who mourn and those who seek to provide comfort in times of sadness. While this book is written from a layperson's point of view, it also includes the specifics for funeral preparations and practical guidance for preparing the home and family to sit shiva.

"A sensitive and perceptive guide to Jewish tradition. Both those who mourn and those who comfort will find it a map to accompany them through the whirlwind."
—*Deborah E. Lipstadt, Emory University*

7" x 9", 320 pp. Quality Paperback, ISBN 1-879045-96-6 **$16.95**

FINDING JOY
A Practical Spiritual Guide to Happiness
by *Dannel I. Schwartz* with *Mark Hass*

Searching for happiness in our modern world of stress and struggle is common; *finding* it is more unusual. This guide explores and explains how to find joy through a time-honored, creative—and surprisingly practical—approach based on the teachings of Jewish mysticism and Kabbalah.

•AWARD WINNER•   "Practical as well as spiritual....excellent illustrative materials....well worth perusing and taking to heart."
—*The American Rabbi*

6" x 9", 192 pp. HC, ISBN 1-879045-53-2 **$19.95**

THE EMPTY CHAIR:
FINDING HOPE & JOY
Timeless Wisdom from a Hasidic Master, Rebbe Nachman of Breslov
Adapted by Moshe Mykoff and the Breslov Research Institute

A "little treasure" of aphorisms and advice for living joyously and spiritually today, written 200 years ago, but startlingly fresh in meaning and use. Challenges and helps us to move from stress and sadness to hope and joy.

•AWARD WINNER•

Teacher, guide and spiritual master—Rebbe Nachman provides vital words of inspiration and wisdom for life today for people of any faith, or of no faith.

"Its words can lift a heavy heart and give inspiration to those facing the problems of everyday life."
—*Community*, Jewish Community Federation of Louisville

4" x 6", 128 pp., 2-color text, Deluxe Paperback, ISBN 1-879045-67-2 **$9.95**

THE DEATH OF DEATH
Resurrection and Immortality in Jewish Thought
by *Neil Gillman*

Noted theologian Neil Gillman explores the original and compelling argument that Judaism, a religion often thought to pay little attention to the afterlife, not only offers us rich ideas on the subject—but delivers a death-blow to death itself. By exploring Jewish thought about death and the afterlife, this fascinating work presents us with challenging new ideas about our lives.

"Enables us to recover our tradition's understanding of the afterlife and breaks through the silence of modern Jewish thought on immortality.... A work of major significance."
—*Rabbi Sheldon Zimmerman, President,*
Hebrew Union College–Jewish Institute of Religion

6" x 9", 336 pp., HC, ISBN 1-879045-61-3 **$23.95**

A HEART OF WISDOM
Making the Jewish Journey from Midlife Through the Elder Years
Edited by *Susan Berrin*

We are all growing older. *A Heart of Wisdom* shows us how to understand our own process of aging—and the aging of those we care about—from a Jewish perspective, from midlife through the elder years.

How does Jewish tradition influence our own aging? How does living, thinking and worshipping as a Jew affect us as we age? How can Jewish tradition help us retain our dignity as we age? Offers insights and enlightenment from Jewish tradition.

"A thoughtfully orchestrated collection of pieces that deal candidly and compassionately with a period of growing concern to us all: midlife through old age."
—*Chaim Potok*

6" x 9", 384 pp. HC, ISBN 1-879045-73-7 **$24.95**

Spiritual Inspiration

HOW TO BE A PERFECT STRANGER
A Guide to Etiquette in Other People's Religious Ceremonies
Edited by *Arthur J. Magida* & *Stuart M. Matlins*
VOL. 1: America's Largest Faiths
VOL. 2: Other Faiths in America
6 x 9, HC, Vol. 1: 432 pp. **$24.95** / Vol. 2: 416 pp. **$24.95**

SELF, STRUGGLE & CHANGE
Family Conflict Stories in Genesis and Their Healing Insights for Our Lives
by *Norman J. Cohen*
6 x 9, HC, 224 pp. PB **$16.95**; HC **$21.95**

BEING GOD'S PARTNER
How to Find the Hidden Link Between Spirituality and Your Work
by *Rabbi Jeffrey K. Salkin*
6 x 9, 192 pp. PB **$16.95**; HC **$19.95**

GOD & THE BIG BANG
Discovering Harmony Between Science & Spirituality
by *Daniel C. Matt*
6 x 9, 216 pp. PB **$16.95**; HC **$21.95**

HEALING OF SOUL, HEALING OF BODY
Spiritual Leaders Unfold the Strength and Solace in Psalms
Edited by *Rabbi Simkha Y. Weintraub, CSW,*
for The Jewish Healing Center
6 x 9, 128 pp. PB **$14.95**

Books by Lawrence Kushner

INVISIBLE LINES OF CONNECTION
Sacred Stories of the Ordinary
5.5 x 8.5, 160 pp. PB $15.95; HC $21.95

HONEY FROM THE ROCK
An Easy Introduction to Jewish Mysticism
6 x 9, 168 pp. PB $14.95

THE BOOK OF WORDS
Talking Spiritual Life, Living Spiritual Talk
6 x 9, 152 pp. Two-color text. HC $21.95

THE BOOK OF LETTERS
A Mystical Hebrew Alphabet
In calligraphy by the author
6 x 9, 80 pp. Two-color text. HC $24.95 Also available in Deluxe ($79.95) and Collector's Editions. ($349.00) *Call for details.*

GOD WAS IN THIS PLACE & I, i DID NOT KNOW
Finding Self, Spirituality & Ultimate Meaning
6 x 9, 192 pp. PB $16.95

THE RIVER OF LIGHT
Spirituality, Judaism, Consciousness
6 x 9, 180 pp. PB $14.95

For ages 9 – 13   ## THE BOOK OF MIRACLES
A Young Person's Guide to Jewish Spiritual Awareness
6 x 9, 96 pp. HC $16.95

Spiritual Inspiration for Children
MULTICULTURAL, NONSECTARIAN, NONDENOMINATIONAL

Books by Sandy Eisenberg Sasso

For ages 4 – 8

GOD'S PAINTBRUSH
full color illustrations by *Annette Compton*
Invites children to encounter God openly in their lives.
11 x 8.5, HC, 32 pp. Illustrated. **$16.95**

IN GOD'S NAME
For ages 4 – 8
full color illustrations by *Phoebe Stone*
A vibrant fable about the search for God's name.
9 x 12, HC, 32 pp. Illustrated. **$16.95**

For ages 8 & up

BUT GOD REMEMBERED
Stories of Women from Creation to the Promised Land
full color illustrations by *Bethanne Andersen*
9 x 12, HC, 32 pp. Illustrated. **$16.95**

A PRAYER FOR THE EARTH
For ages 4 – 8
The Story of Naamah, Noah's Wife
full color illustrations by *Bethanne Andersen*
9 x 12, HC, 32 pp. Illustrated. **$16.95**

For all ages

THE 11TH COMMANDMENT
Wisdom from Our Children
by *The Children of America*
with full color illustrations
8 x 10, HC, 48 pp. Illustrated. **$16.95**

SHARING BLESSINGS
For ages 6 – 10
Children's Stories for Exploring the Spirit of the Jewish Holidays
by *Rahel Musleah* and *Rabbi Michael Klayman*
full color illustrations by *Mary O'Keefe Young*
8.5 x 11, HC, 64 pp. Illustrated. **$18.95**

(cut along dotted line) **ORDER FORM**

On a separate piece of paper, please list the titles of the books you want to order & the number of copies. Please add $3.50 s/h for 1st book, $2.00 ea. add'l. book   TOTAL $ _____

Check enclosed for $ _____ *payable to:* JEWISH LIGHTS Publishing

Charge my credit card: ☐ MasterCard ☐ Visa

Credit Card # _____ Expires _____

Name on card _____

Signature _____ Phone (_____) _____

Name _____

Street _____

City / State / Zip _____

Phone, fax, or mail to: JEWISH LIGHTS Publishing
P.O. Box 237, Sunset Farm Offices, Route 4, Woodstock, Vermont 05091
Tel (802) 457-4000   Fax (802) 457-4004   www.jewishlights.com
Credit card orders (800) 962-4544 (9AM–5PM ET Monday–Friday)
Generous discounts on quantity orders. SATISFACTION GUARANTEED. Prices subject to change.
AVAILABLE FROM BETTER BOOKSTORES. *TRY YOUR BOOKSTORE FIRST.*